Sweaters for Men

PLANET

Original edition first published in 1985 under the title,
Männer Pullover, by Mosaik Verlag GmbH, Neumarkter Strasse 18,
D-8000 München 80, West Germany.

Photoset in Palatino by Phoenix Photosetting, Chatham, Kent
Printed and bound in Singapore for the publishers
W.H. Allen & Co Plc, 44 Hill Street, London W1X 8LB

ISBN 1–85227–005–5

Every effort has been made to trace UK suppliers/agents for the foreign yarns specified in the
patterns appearing in the original German edition of the book, *Männer Pullover*. Where this
has not been possible, substitute UK yarns have been specified and the patterns adapted
accordingly.

Please note that the colours reproduced in the illustrations may vary from the actual yarn shades
specified due to the limitations of the printing process. Readers are also advised that the yarn
shade numbers detailed in the patterns are to the best of our knowledge correct at time of going
to press, but are subject to change from time to time.

ACKNOWLEDGEMENTS

For the adaptation and translation of the knitting patterns, and for the design and creation of the
pattern on page 53: Erika Harrison.

For their assistance in supplying yarn:
Avocet Hand Knitting Yarns, Hammond Associates Ltd, Harrogate, North Yorkshire (Avocet); Carter
& Parker Ltd, Guiseley, Yorkshire (Wendy Wools); French Wools Ltd, London (Pingouin); Patons &
Baldwins Ltd, Darlington, Co. Durham (Jaeger and Patons & Baldwins); Phildar (UK) Ltd,
Northampton (Phildar); Richard Poppleton & Sons Ltd, Horbury, Wakefield, Yorkshire (Richard
Poppleton); Scheepjeswol (UK) Ltd, Redditch, Worcestershire (Scheepjeswol); Smallwares Ltd, London
(Schaffhauser); J. Henry Smith Ltd, Calverton, Nottingham (Lang); Viking Wools Ltd, Ambleside,
Cumbria (Berger du Nord and Falkland Islands); Yeoman Yarns, Kibworth, Leicestershire (H.E.C.)

For the use of colour photographs:
Afra GmbH, Hamburg (Pingouin Wool); Max Austermann GmbH & Co, Wuppertal; Laines Berger du
Nord Deutschland GmbH, Düsseldorf; Garnimport H. Ernst GmbH, Renningen (H.E.C. Wool); Italana
Handels GmbH, Ingolstadt; Junghans Wollversand GmbH & Co KG, Aachen; Kammgarnspinnerei
Wilhelmshaven AG, Wilhelmshaven (Hübner Wool); Klaus Koch GmbH, Köln (KKK Wool);
Koninklijke D.S. van Schuppen, Veenendaal/Niederlande (Scheepjeswol); Lang & Cie,
Reiden/Schweiz; Phildar Wolle GmbH, Wiesbaden; Scaioni's Studio, London; Schachenmayr, Mann &
Cie GmbH, Salach; Schoeller Albers AG, Schaffhausen/Schweiz (Schaffhauser Wool); Schoeller Eitorf
AG, Eitorf/Sieg (Esslinger Wool and Schoeller Wool); Seiden und Garn GmbH, Freiburg/Br. (Jaeger
Wool and Patons Wool); Sjöberg Wolle Handelsges. mbH, Wildeshausen

Cover picture: **Crossed Stitches** sweater (left) in
Falkland Islands Tweed and **Giant Cable** sweater
(right) in Berger du Nord Lima

CONTENTS

HIGHLY PATTERNED

MATERIALS

H.E.C. Aarlan Royal
Shade No. 4285 Turquoise   15:   16:   17: 40g balls
Pair each 3mm and 4mm knitting needles.

MEASUREMENTS

	92/97:	97/102:	102/107:	cm
To fit chest	36/38:	38/40:	40/42:	in.
Actual measurements	104:	108:	112:	cm
	41:	42½:	44:	in.
Length	68:	71:	71:	cm
	26¾:	28:	28:	in.
Sleeve length	51:	53:	53:	cm
	20:	20¾:	20¾:	in.

TENSION

22 sts and 34 rows = 10cm [4in.] over patt on 4mm needles.

ABBREVIATIONS

K = knit; P = purl; st(s) = stitch(es); patt = pattern; rep = repeat; inc = increase; beg = beginning; alt = alternate; dec = decrease; sl = slip; cm = centimetres; in. = inches.

The patt repeat [worked over 34 sts].
1st row. [K1, P1] twice, K4, [P1, K1] 3 times, P1, K5, [P1, K1] 3 times, P1, K4, P1, K1, P1.
2nd row. P1, K1, P4, [K1, P1] 3 times, K1, P7, [K1, P1] 3 times, K1, P4, K1, P1, K1.
3rd row. K1, P1, K4, [P1, K1] 3 times, P1, K9, [P1, K1] 3 times, P1, K4, P1.
4th row. P4, [K1, P1] 3 times, K1, P5, K1, P5, [K1, P1] 3 times, K1, P4, K1.
5th row. K4, [P1, K1] 3 times, P1, K5, P1, K1, P1, K5, [P1, K1] 3 times, P1, K3.
6th row. P2, [K1, P1] 3 times, K1, P5, [K1, P1] twice, K1, P5, [K1, P1] 3 times, K1, P3.
7th row. K2, [P1, K1] 3 times, P1, K5, [P1, K1] 3 times, P1, K5, [P1, K1] 4 times.
8th row. [K1, P1] 3 times, K1, P5, [K1, P1] 4 times, K1, P5, [K1, P1] 4 times.
9th row. [P1, K1] 3 times, P1, K5, [P1, K1] 5 times, P1, K5, [P1, K1] 3 times.
10th row. [K1, P1] twice, K1, P5, [K1, P1] 6 times, K1, P5, [K1, P1] 3 times.
11th row. [P1, K1] twice, P1, K5, [P1, K1] 7 times, P1, K5, [P1, K1] twice.
12th row. K1, P1, K1, P5, [K1, P1] 3 times, K1, P3, [K1, P1] 3 times, K1, P5, [K1, P1] twice.
13th row. P1, K1, P1, K5, [P1, K1] 3 times, P1, K5, [P1, K1] 3 times, P1, K5, P1, K1.
14th row. K1, P5, [K1, P1] 3 times, K1, P7, [K1, P1] 3 times, K1, P5, K1, P1.
15th row. P1, K5, [P1, K1] 3 times, P1, K4, P1, K4, [P1, K1] 3 times, P1, K5.
16th row. P4, [K1, P1] 3 times, K1, P4, K1, P1, K1, P4, [K1, P1] 3 times, K1, P5.
17th row. K4, [P1, K1] 3 times, P1, K4, [P1, K1] twice, P1, K4, [P1, K1] 3 times, P1, K3.
18th row. P2, [K1, P1] 3 times, K1, P4, [K1, P1] 3 times, K1, P4, [K1, P1] 3 times, K1, P3.
19th row. As 17th row.
20th row. As 16th row.
21st row. As 15th row.
22nd row. As 14th row.
23rd row. As 13th row.
24th row. As 12th row.
25th row. As 11th row.

26th row. As 10th row.
27th row. As 9th row.
28th row. As 8th row.
29th row. As 7th row.
30th row. As 6th row.
31st row. As 5th row.
32nd row. As 4th row.
33rd row. As 3rd row.
34th row. As 2nd row.
These 34 rows form the patt.

BACK

With 3mm needles cast on 95(99:103) sts.
1st row. K2, ★ P1, K1, rep from ★ to
last st, K1.
2nd row. ★ K1, P1, rep from ★ to last st, K1.
Rep 1st and 2nd rows for 7cm [2¾in.]
ending with 1st row.
Next row. Rib 4(6:8), inc in next st, ★ rib
4, inc in next st, rep from ★ to last
5(7:9) sts, rib to end. [113(117:121) sts.]

Change to 4mm needles and patt.

Note.
Figures in round brackets at beg and end
of rows refer to the larger sizes.

1st row. K2, P1, K1, P1 (K4, P1, K1, P1)
(K1, P1, K4, P1, K1, P1); rep 34 sts of
patt 3 times; [K1, P1] twice, K2 ([K1, P1]
twice, K4) ([K1, P1] twice, K4, P1, K1).
2nd row. P3, K1, P1, K1 (K1, P4, K1, P1,
K1) (K1, P1, K1, P4, K1, P1, K1); rep
34 sts of patt 3 times; P1, K1, P3 (P1, K1,
P4, K1) (P1, K1, P4, K1, P1, K1).
3rd row. K4, P1 (K1, P1, K4, P1) ([K1,
P1] twice, K4, P1); rep 34 sts of patt 3
times, K1, P1, K4 (K1, P1, K4, P1, K1)
(K1, P1, K4, [P1, K1] twice).
4th row. K1, P4, K1 (K1, P1, K1, P4, K1)
([K1, P1] twice, K1, P4, K1); rep 34 sts of
patt 3 times; P4, K1 (P4, K1, P1, K1) (P4,
[K1, P1] twice, K1).
5th row. K1, P1, K3 ([K1, P1] twice, K3)
([K1, P1] 3 times, K3); rep 34 sts of patt 3
times; K4, P1, K1 (K4, [P1, K1] twice)
(K4, [P1, K1] 3 times).
6th row. K1, P1, K1, P3 ([K1, P1] twice, K1,

P3) ([K1, P1] 3 times, K1, P3); rep 34 sts of
patt 3 times; P2, K1, P1, K1 (P2, [K1, P1]
twice, K1) (P2, [K1, P1] 3 times, K1).
7th row. [K1, P1] twice, K1 ([K1, P1] 3
times, K1) ([K1, P1] 4 times, K1); rep
34 sts of patt 3 times; K2, [P1, K1] twice
(K2, [P1, K1] 3 times) (K2, [P1, K1] 4
times).
8th row. [K1, P1] 3 times ([K1, P1] 4
times) (P2, [K1, P1] 4 times); rep 34 sts of
patt 3 times; [K1, P1] twice, K1 ([K1, P1]
3 times, K1) ([K1, P1] 3 times, K1, P2).
9th row. [K1, P1] twice, K1 ([K1, P1] 3
times, K1) (K3, [P1, K1] 3 times); rep
34 sts of patt 3 times; [P1, K1] 3 times
([P1, K1] 4 times) ([P1, K1] 4 times, K2).
10th row. [K1, P1] 3 times (P2, [K1, P1] 3
times) (P4 [K1, P1] 3 times); rep 34 sts of
patt 3 times; [K1, P1] twice, K1 ([K1, P1]
twice, K1, P2) ([K1, P1] twice, K1, P4).
11th row. K1, [P1, K1] twice (K3, [P1,
K1] twice) (K5, [P1, K1] twice); rep 34 sts
of patt 3 times; [P1, K1] 3 times ([P1, K1]
twice, P1, K3) ([P1, K1] twice, P1, K5).
12th row. P2, [K1, P1] twice (P4, [K1, P1]
twice) (K1, P5, [K1, P1] twice); rep 34 sts
of patt 3 times; K1, P1, K1, P2 (K1, P1,
K1, P4) (K1, P1, K1, P5, K1).
13th row. K3, P1, K1 (K5, P1, K1) (K1,
P1, K5, P1, K1); rep 34 sts of patt 3 times;
P1, K1, P1, K3 (P1, K1, P1, K5) (P1, K1,
P1, K5, P1, K1).
14th row. P4, K1, P1 (K1, P5, K1, P1)
(K1, P1, K1, P5, K1, P1); rep 34 sts of
patt 3 times; K1, P4 (K1, P5, K1) (K1, P5,
K1, P1, K1).
15th row. K5 (K1, P1, K5) ([K1, P1] twice,
K5); rep 34 sts of patt 3 times; P1, K5 (P1,
K5, P1, K1) (P1, K5, [P1, K1] twice).
16th row. K1, P5 (K1, P1, K1, P5) ([K1,
P1] twice, K1, P5); repeat 34 sts of patt 3
times; P4, K1 (P4, K1, P1, K1) (P4, [K1,
P1] twice, K1).
17th row. K1, P1, K3 ([K1, P1] twice, K3)
([K1, P1] 3 times, K3); rep 34 sts of patt 3
times; K4, P1, K1 (K4, [P1, K1] twice)
(K4, [P1, K1] 3 times).
18th row. K1, P1, K1, P3 ([K1, P1] twice,
K1, P3) ([K1, P1] 3 times, K1, P3); rep 34 sts
of patt 3 times; P2, K1, P1, K1 (P2, [K1, P1]
twice, K1) (P2, [K1, P1] 3 times, K1).

19th row. As 17th row.
20th row. As 16th row.
21st row. As 15th row.
22nd row. As 14th row.
23rd row. As 13th row.
24th row. As 12th row.
25th row. As 11th row.
26th row. As 10th row.
27th row. As 9th row.
28th row. As 8th row.
29th row. As 7th row.
30th row. As 6th row.
31st row. As 5th row.
32nd row. As 4th row.
33rd row. As 3rd row.
34th row. As 2nd row.
These 34 rows form patt for remainder of back.
Work until back measures 67(69:69)cm [26¼(27:27)in.] from commencement, ending with a wrong side row.

Shape shoulders.
Cast off at beg of next and following rows, 12(13:13) sts twice, 12(12:13) sts twice, and 12(13:13) sts twice.
Cast off 41(41:43) remaining sts for back of neck.

FRONT

Follow instructions for back until front is 24 rows less than back to start of shoulders.

Shape neck.
Next row. Patt 52(54:55) sts, cast off 9(9:11) sts, patt to end.
Continue on last set of sts.
Work 1 row.
** Cast off 3 sts at beg of next row, and 2 sts at beg of 2 following alt rows; now dec 1 st at beg of every alt row until 36(38:39) sts remain, ending at armhole edge.
Shape shoulder as back.
With wrong side facing rejoin yarn to remaining sts at neck edge and follow instructions for other side from ** to end.

SLEEVES

With 3mm needles cast on 53(53:53) sts.
Work 6cm [2¼in.] in rib as back, ending with 1st row.
Next row. Rib 4(1:1), inc in next st, * rib 2, inc in next st, rep from * to last 3(0:0) sts, rib 3(0:0). [69(71:71) sts.]

Change to 4mm needles and patt.
1st row. K3(4:4), [P1, K1] 3 times, P1, K4, P1, K1, P1; work the 34 sts of patt; [K1, P1] twice, K4, [P1, K1] 3 times, P1, K3(4:4).
Continue in patt as set. Work 6 rows.
Inc 1 st at each end of next row, and then every 6th row until 81(85:85) sts, and then every 8th row until 107(111:111) sts are on the needle.
Work until sleeve measures 51(53:53)cm [20(20¾:20¾)in.] from commencement, ending with a wrong side row.

Shape top.
Cast off 9 sts at beg of next 6(4:4) rows, and 10 sts at beg of following 4(6:6) rows.
Cast off 13(15:15) remaining sts.

MAKING UP

Press each piece lightly, following instructions on ball band.
Join right shoulder seam.

Neck border.
With 3mm needles and right side facing, pick up and K 60(62:64) sts evenly along front neck edge, and 42(44:44) sts along back neck edge.
Work 22 rows in K1, P1, rib.
Cast off loosely in rib.
Join left shoulder and neck border seam.
Fold neck border in half on to wrong side and sl st loosely to picked up edge.
Place a marker 24(25:25)cm [9½(10:10)in.] on each side of shoulder seams to mark depth of armholes.
Join cast off edge of sleeves to armhole edges.
Join side and sleeve seams. Press seams.

MODERN SHAWL COLLAR

MATERIALS

Jaeger Luxury Spun

1st shade 409 Barley	8:	9:	10:	50g balls
2nd shade 420 Mole	6:	6:	7:	50g balls

Pair of 3¾mm, and a pair of long 4½mm double pointed knitting needles.

MEASUREMENTS

To fit chest	97:	102:	107:	cm
	38:	40:	42:	in.
Actual measurements	107:	112:	117:	cm
	42:	44:	46:	in.
Length	65:	65:	66:	cm
	25½:	25½:	26:	in.
Sleeve length	53:	54.5:	54.5:	cm
	21:	21½:	21½:	in.

TENSION

20 sts and 36 rows = 10cm [4in.] over patt on 4½mm needles.

ABBREVIATIONS

K = knit; P = purl; st(s) = stitch(es); A = 1st shade; B = 2nd shade; M1 = inc 1 st by picking up strand between last st worked and next st, and work into back of it; rep = repeat; patt = pattern; inc = increase; cm = centimetres; in. = inches.

BACK

★★ With 3¾mm needles and A, cast on 94(98:104) sts.
Work 7cm [2¾in.] in K1, P1, rib.
Next row. Rib 3(5:8), M1, ★ rib 8, M1, rep from ★ to last 3(5:8) sts, rib to end.
[106(110:116) sts.]

Change to 4½mm needles.

Commence patt.
1st row [right side]. With B: K1, ★ K1, P1, rep from ★ to last st, K1. Do not turn, but return to beginning of row.
2nd row [right side]. With A: K1, ★ P1, K1, rep from ★ to last st, K1. Turn.

3rd row [wrong side]. With B: as 1st row. Do not turn but return to beginning of row.
4th row [wrong side]. With A: as 2nd row. Turn.
These 4 rows form the patt. ★★
Work until back measures 65(65:66)cm [25½(25½:26)in.] from commencement.
Cast off in patt.

FRONT

Follow instructions for back from ★★ to ★★.
Work until front measures 45(45:46)cm [17½(17½:18)in.] from commencement.

Shape for neck.
Next row. Patt 33(35:38) sts, cast off 40 sts, patt to end.

Continue on last set of sts.
Work until front measures same as back to shoulder.
Cast off.
Rejoin yarn to remaining sts and complete to match other side.

MODERN SHAWL COLLAR

SLEEVES

With 3¾mm needles and A, cast on 52(52:52) sts and work 6cm [2½in.] in K1, P1, rib.
Next row. * Rib 4, M1, rep from * to last 4 sts, rib 4. [64 sts.]

Change to 4½mm needles and patt.
Work 8 rows.
Now working the new sts in patt, inc 1 st at each end of next row, and then every 8th row until 100(104:104) sts are on the needle.
Work until sleeve measures 53(54.5:54.5)cm [21(21½:21½)in.] from commencement.
Cast off.

COLLAR

With 3¾mm needles and A, cast on 159 sts.
1st row. K2, * P1, K1, rep from * to last st, K1.

2nd row. * K1, P1, rep from * to last st, K1.
Rep 1st and 2nd rows for 21cm [8¼in.].
Cast off loosely in rib.

MAKING UP

Press each piece lightly, following instructions on ball band.
Join shoulder seams.
Sew cast on edge of collar to side and back neck edges.
Join side edges of collar to cast off sts at front with left side overlapping right side.
Place a marker 26(27:27)cm [10¼(10½:10½)in.] on each side of shoulder seams to mark depth of armholes.
Join cast off edge of sleeves to armhole edges.
Join side and sleeve seams.
Press seams.

CROSSED STITCHES

MATERIALS

Falkland Islands Tweed shade Roan	16:	16:	17:	50g balls

Pair each 4mm and 5mm knitting needles. A cable needle.

MEASUREMENTS

To fit chest	92/97:	99/104:	107/112:	cm
	36/38:	39/41:	42/44:	in.
Actual measurements	107:	114.5:	122:	cm
	42:	45:	48:	in.
Length	65:	67:	69:	cm
	25½:	26¼:	27:	in.
Sleeve length	48:	49:	50:	cm
	18¾:	19¼:	19½:	in.

TENSION

17 sts and 24 rows = 10cm [4in.] over st. st. on 5mm needles.

ABBREVIATIONS

K = knit; P = purl; st(s) = stitch(es); st. st. = stocking stitch; C4F [cable 4 front] = slip next 2 sts on to cable needle and hold at front, K2, then K2 from cable needle; C3F [cable 3 front] = slip next 2 sts on to cable needle and hold at front, P next st, then K2 from cable needle; C3B [cable 3 back] = slip next st on to cable needle and hold at back, K2, then P st from cable needle; M1 = increase 1 st by picking up strand between last st worked and next st, and work into back of it; rep = repeat; patt = pattern; dec = decrease; beg = beginning; inc = increase; sl 1 = slip 1; cm = centimetres; in. = inches.

BACK

With 4mm needles cast on 85(91:95) sts.
1st row. K2, * P1, K1, rep from * to last st, K1.

2nd row. * K1, P1, rep from * to last st, K1. Rep 1st and 2nd rows for 6.5cm [2½in.], ending with 1st row.

Change to 5mm needles.
Next row. P3(6:5), M1, * P8(8:7), M1, rep from * to last 2(5:6) sts, P to end. [96(102:108) sts.]

Commence 1st patt.
1st row. P7(10:13), K4, * P9, K4, rep from * to last 7(10:13) sts, P to end.
2nd row. K7(10:13), P4, * K9, P4, rep from * to last 7(10:13) sts, K to end.
3rd row. P7(10:13), C4F, * P9, C4F, rep from * to last 7(10:13) sts, P to end.
4th row. As 2nd row.
5th to 8th rows. Rep 1st to 4th rows.
9th row. K.
10th row. P.
11th row. K7(10:13), C4F, * K9, C4F, rep from * to last 7(10:13) sts, K to end.
12th row. P.
Rep 1st to 12th rows 4 times more.

Commence 2nd patt.
1st row. P7(10:13), K4, * P9, K4, rep from * to last 7(10:13) sts, P7(10:13).
2nd and following alt rows. K all K sts and P all P sts.
3rd row. P6(9:12), C3B, C3F, * P7, C3B, C3F, rep from * to last 6(9:12) sts, P to end.

5th row. P5(8:11), C3B, P2, C3F, ★ P5, C3B, P2, C3F, rep from ★ to last 5(8:11) sts, P to end.
7th row. P5(8:11), K2, P4, K2, ★ P5, K2, P4, K2, rep from ★ to last 5(8:11) sts, P to end.
9th row. As 7th row.
11th row. P5(8:11), C3F, P2, C3B, ★ P5, C3F, P2, C3B, rep from ★ to last 5(8:11) sts, P to end.
13th row. P6(9:12), C3F, C3B, ★ P7, C3F, C3B, rep from ★ to last 6(9:12) sts, P to end.
15th row. P7(10:13), C4F, ★ P9, C4F, rep from ★ to last 7(10:13) sts, P to end.
16th row. As 2nd row.
These 16 rows form patt.
Work until back measures 63(65:67)cm [24¾(25½:26¼)in.] from commencement, ending with a wrong side row.

Shape neck.
Next row. Patt 35(38:41) sts, cast off 26 sts, patt to end.

Continue on last set of sts.
Dec 1 st at neck edge on next 2 rows.
Work 1 row.
Cast off 33(36:39) remaining sts.
With wrong side facing, rejoin yarn to remaining sts at neck edge and complete to match other side.

FRONT

Follow instructions for back until work measures 44(46:48)cm [17¼(18:18¾)in.] from commencement, ending with a wrong side row.

Shape neck.
Next row. Patt 38(41:44) sts, cast off 20 sts, patt to end.

Continue on last set of sts.
Work 7 rows.
Dec 1 st at beg of next row, and then

every 8th row until 33(36:39) sts remain.
Work until front measures same as back to shoulder, ending with a wrong side row.
Cast off.
With wrong side facing, rejoin yarn to remaining sts at neck edge and complete to match other side.

SLEEVES

With 4mm needles cast on 41(43:43) sts and work 8cm [3¼in.] in rib as back, ending with 1st row.

Change to 5mm needles.
Next row. P2(3:1), M1, ★ P2, M1, rep from ★ to last 3(4:2) sts, P3(4:2). [60(62:64) sts.]

Commence 1st patt.
1st row. P2(3:4), K4, ★ P9, K4, rep from ★ to last 2(3:4) sts, P2(3:4).

Continue in 1st patt as set.
Work 5 rows.
Now working the new sts in patt, inc 1 st at each end of next row, and then alternately on 4th and 6th rows until 82(84:86) sts are on the needle and then every 4th row until 94(96:98) sts are on the needle.
Work 3 rows.
84 rows should now be worked in 1st patt.

Continue in 2nd patt.
Work 16(18:20) rows, and at the same time inc 1 st at each end of next row, and then the 3 following 4th rows.
Cast off.

COLLAR

With 5mm needles cast on 108 sts.
Work 12cm [4¾in.] in garter st [every row K].

Continue as follows:

1st row. K to last 16 sts, turn.
2nd row. Sl 1, K to last 16 sts, turn.
3rd row. Sl 1, K to last 33 sts, turn.
4th row. Sl 1, K to last 33 sts, turn.
5th row. Sl 1, K to end.
6th row. K to end.
Cast off.

MAKING UP

Press each piece lightly, following instructions on ball band.
Join shoulder seams.
Place a marker 28.5(30:30)cm [11¼(11¾:11¾)in.] on each side of shoulder seams to mark depth of armholes. Join cast off edge of sleeves to armhole edges. Join side and sleeve seams.
Sew cast off edge of collar to neck edge, with side edges overlapping at front as shown.
Press seams.

MATERIALS

Lang La Paz

Shade No. 7776 Blue Marl	14:	15:	16:	16:	40g balls

Pair each 3¼mm and 4½mm knitting needles.

MEASUREMENTS

To fit chest	92/97:	97/102:	102/107:	107/112:	cm
	36/38:	38/40:	40/42:	42/44:	in.
Actual measurements	102:	107:	112:	117:	cm
	40:	42:	44:	46:	in.
Length	67:	67:	71:	71:	cm
	26½:	26½:	28:	28:	in.
Sleeve length	50:	50:	50:	50:	cm
	19¾:	19¾:	19¾:	19¾:	in.

TENSION

22 sts and 28 rows = 10cm [4in.] over patt on 4½mm needles.

ABBREVIATIONS

K = knit; P = purl; st(s) = stitch(es); rep = repeat; inc = increase; patt = pattern; st. st. = stocking stitch; alt = alternate; cm = centimetres; in. = inches.

BACK

With 3¼mm needles cast on 101(107:113:119) sts.
1st row. K2, * P1, K1, rep from * to last st, K1.
2nd row. * K1, P1, rep from * to last st, K1.
Rep 1st and 2nd rows for 7cm [2¾in.] ending with 1st row.
Next row. P5(8:6:9), inc in next st, * P9(9:10:10), inc in next st, rep from * to last 5(8:7:10) sts. [111(117:123:129) sts.]

Change to 4½mm needles and patt.

1st and 3rd sizes.
1st row. K1, [P3, K3] 9(10) times, P1, [K3, P3] 9(10) times, K1.
2nd row. K all K sts and P all P sts.
3rd row. K1, [P2, K3, P1] 9(10) times, P1, [P1, K3, P2] 9(10) times, K1.
5th row. K1, [P1, K3, P2] 9(10) times, P1, [P2, K3, P1] 9(10) times, K1.
7th row. K1, [K3, P3] 9(10) times, K1, [P3, K3] 9(10) times, K1.
9th row. K1, [K2, P3, K1] 9(10) times, K1, [K1, P3, K2] 9(10) times, K1.
11th row. K1, [K1, P3, K2] 9(10) times, K1, [K2, P3, K1] 9(10) times, K1.
12th row. As 2nd row.

2nd and 4th sizes.
1st row. K1, [K3, P3] 9(10) times, K3, P1, K3, [P3, K3] 9(10) times, K1.
2nd and following alt rows. K all K sts and P all P sts.
3rd row. K1, [K2, P3, K1] 9(10) times, K2, P3, K2, [K1, P3, K2] 9(10) times, K1.
5th row. K1, [K1, P3, K2] 9(10) times, K1, P5, K1, [K2, P3, K1] 9(10) times, K1.
7th row. K1, [P3, K3] 9(10) times, P3, K1, P3, [K3, P3] 9(10) times, K1.
9th row. K1, [P2, K3, P1] 9(10) times, P2, K3, P2, [P1, K3, P2] 9(10) times, K1.
11th row. K1, [P1, K3, P2] 9(10) times, P1, K5, P1, [P2, K3, P1] 9(10) times, K1.
12th row. As 2nd row.
These 12 rows form patt.

Work until the 12th row of the 9th (9th:10th:10th) patt has been completed. Now work 54 more rows, and *at the same time* work 1 st more at each side of centre in st. st. on next and every following alt row for yoke, keeping the remainder in patt.

Change to 3¼mm needles and work 3cm [1¼in.] in rib as welt.

Cast off in rib.

FRONT

Work as back.

SLEEVES

With 3¾mm needles cast on 53(53:57:57) sts.

Work 7cm [2¾in.] in rib as back.

Next row. P3(3:2:2), inc in next st, ★ P2, inc in next st, rep from ★ to last 4(4:3:3) sts, P to end. [69(69:75:75) sts.]

Change to 4½mm needles.

1st row [1st and 2nd sizes only]. K1, [K3, P3] 5 times, K3, P1, K3, [P3, K3] 5 times, K1.

1st row [3rd and 4th sizes only]. K1, [P3, K3] 6 times, P1, [K3, P3] 6 times, K1.

Continue in patt as set.

Work 5 more rows.

Now working the new sts in patt, inc 1 st at each end of next row, and then every 6th row until 91(91:97:97) sts and then every 4th row until 113(113:119:119) sts are on the needle.

Work until sleeve measures 50cm [19¾in.] from commencement.

Cast off in patt.

MAKING UP

Press each piece lightly, following instructions on ball band.

Join shoulder seams, leaving neck open as required.

Place a marker 27(27:28:28)cm [10½(10½:11:11)in.] on each side of shoulder seams to mark depth of armholes.

Join cast off edge of sleeves to armhole edges.

Join side and sleeve seams.

Press seams.

Picture opposite: **Axis Symmetry** sweater in Lang La Paz wool

18 ARAN

MATERIALS

Avocet Aran shade 400 Aran   14:   15:   16:   50g balls

Pair each 4mm and 5mm knitting needles. A cable needle.

MEASUREMENTS

To fit chest	97:	102:	107:	cm
	38:	40:	42:	in.
Actual measurements	107:	112:	117:	cm
	42:	44:	46:	in.
Length	68:	68:	68:	cm
	26¾:	26¾:	26¾:	in.
Sleeve length	54:	54:	54:	cm
	21¼:	21¼:	21¼:	in.

TENSION

19 sts and 22 rows = 10cm [4in.] over patt on 5mm needles.

ABBREVIATIONS

K = knit; P = purl; st(s) = stitch(es); patt = pattern; C5 [cable 5] = sl next 2 sts on to cable needle and hold at front, K2, P1, then K2 sts from cable needle; C3B [cable 3 back] = sl next st on to cable needle and hold at back, K2, then P 1 st from cable needle; C3F = sl next 2 sts on to cable needle and hold at front, P1, then K2 sts from cable needle; alt = alternate; M1 = inc 1 st by picking up strand between last st worked and next st on needle and work into back of it; tb1 = through back of loop; rep = repeat; C4B [cable 4 back] = sl next 2 sts on to cable needle and hold at back, K2, then K2 from cable needle; C4F [cable 4 front] = sl next 2 sts on to cable needle and hold at front, K2, then K2 from cable needle; dec = decrease; sl = slip; inc = increase; cm = centimetres; in. = inches.

THE DIAMOND PANEL [REFERRED TO AS PATT 27].

1st row. P11, K2, P1, K2, P11.

2nd and all even rows. K all K sts, and P all P sts.
3rd row. P11, C5, P11.
5th row. P10, C3B, P1, C3F, P10.
7th row. P9, C3B, P1, K1, P1, C3F, P9.
9th row. P8, C3B, [P1, K1] twice, P1, C3F, P8.
11th row. P7, C3B, [P1, K1] 3 times, P1, C3F, P7.
Continue in this way having 1 st less at each side in P fabric, and 2 sts more in moss st in the centre on every alt row until there are 2 sts at each side in P fabric, and 17 sts in moss st, ending with a wrong side row.
25th row. P2, K2, [P1, K1] 9 times, P1, K2, P2.
27th row. P2, C3F, [P1, K1] 8 times, P1, C3B, P2.
29th row. P3, C3F, [P1, K1] 7 times, P1, C3B, P3.
Continue in this way having 1 st more at each side in P fabric and 2 sts less in moss st on every alt row until on the 41st row there are 10 sts at each side in P fabric, and 1 st in the moss st panel, ending with a wrong side row.
42nd row. As 2nd row.
The 3rd to 42nd rows form the patt.

FRONT

★★ With 4mm needles cast on 89(93:97) sts.
1st row. K2, ★ P1, K1, rep from ★ to last st, K1.
2nd row. ★ K1, P1, rep from ★ to last st, K1.
Rep 1st and 2nd rows for 7cm [2¾in.] ending with 1st row.

Change to 5mm needles.
Next row. K6(8:3), M1, ★ K7, M1, rep from ★ to last 6(8:3) sts, K to end. [101(105:111) sts.]

Continue in patt.
1st row. P4(6:9), K2 tbl, P2, K4, P2, K1 tbl, P2, K8, P2, K1 tbl, P2, K4, P2, K1 tbl, *patt 27*, K1 tbl, P2, K4, P2, K1 tbl, P2, K8, P2, K1 tbl, P2, K4, P2, K2 tbl, P4(6:9).
2nd and all even rows. K all K sts and P all P sts.
3rd row. P4(6:9), K2 tbl, P2, C4B, P2, K1 tbl, P2, C4F, C4B, P2, K1 tbl, P2, C4B, P2, K1 tbl, *patt 27*, K1 tbl, P2, C4F, P2, K1 tbl, P2, C4F, C4B, P2, K1 tbl, P2, C4F, P2, K2 tbl, P4(6:9).
5th row. P4(6:9), K2 tbl, P2, K4, P2, K1 tbl, P2, K2, C4B, K2, P2, K1 tbl, P2, K4, P2, K1 tbl, *patt 27*, K1 tbl, P2, K4, P2, K1 tbl, P2, K2, C4F, K2, P2, K1 tbl, P2, K4, P2, K2 tbl, P4(6:9).
7th row. P4(6:9), K2 tbl, P2, C4B, P2, K1 tbl, P2, C4B, C4F, P2, K1 tbl, P2, C4B, P2, K1 tbl, *patt 27*, K1 tbl, P2, C4F, P2, K1 tbl, P2, C4B, C4F, P2, K1 tbl, P2, C4F, P2, K2 tbl, P4(6:9).
9th row. P4(6:9), K2 tbl, P2, K4, P2, K1 tbl, P2, K8, P2, K1 tbl, P2, K4, P2, K1 tbl, *patt 27*, K1 tbl, P2, K4, P2, K1 tbl, P2, K8, P2, K1 tbl, P2, K4, P2, K2 tbl, P4(6:9).
11th row. P4(6:9), K2 tbl, P2, C4B, P2, K1 tbl, P2, K8, P2, K1 tbl, P2, C4B, P2, K1 tbl, *patt 27*, K1 tbl, P2, C4F, P2, K1 tbl, P2, K8, P2, K1 tbl, P2, C4F, P2, K2 tbl, P4(6:8).
13th row. As 9th row.

15th row. As 11th row.
16th row. As 2nd row.
These 16 rows form patt for remainder of front.
Work until the 4th row of the 4th diamond patt has been completed. ★★

Shape neck.
Next row. Patt 40(42:44) sts, cast off 21(21:23) sts, patt to end.
Continue on last set of sts.
Dec 1 st at neck edge on next 10 rows.
Cast off remaining 30(32:34) sts.
Rejoin yarn to remaining sts at neck edge and complete to match other side.

BACK

Follow instructions for front from ★★ to ★★.
Work 8 more rows.

Shape back of neck.
Next row. Patt 32(34:36) sts, cast off 37(37:39) sts, patt to end.
Continue on last set of sts.
Dec 1 st at neck edge on next 2 rows.
Cast off remaining sts.
Rejoin yarn to remaining sts at neck edge and complete to match other side.

SLEEVES

With 4mm needles cast on 44(46:46) sts and work 7cm [2¾in.] in rib as front, ending with 1st row.

Change to 5mm needles.
Next row. K1(2:2), M1, ★ K3, M1, rep from ★ to last 1(2:2) sts, K1(2:2). [59(61:61) sts.]

Continue in patt.
1st row. K4(5:5), P2, K1 tbl, P2, K4, P2, K1 tbl, *patt 27*, K1 tbl, P2, K4, P2, K1 tbl, P2, K4(5:5).

Continue in patt as set.
Work 5 more rows.
Now working the new sts in patt, inc 1 st

at each end of next row, and then every 6th row until 89(93:93) sts are on the needle.
Work until sleeve measures 54cm [21¼in.] from commencement.
Cast off loosely.

MAKING UP

Press each piece lightly, following instructions on ball band.
Join right shoulder seam.

Neck border.
With 4mm needles and right side facing, pick up and K 86(86:90) sts along neck edge. Work 3cm [1¼in.] in K1, P1, rib. Cast off in rib.
Join left shoulder and neck border seams. Place a marker 23.5(25:25)cm [9¼(9¾:9¾)in.] on each side of shoulder seams to mark depth of armholes. Join cast off edge of sleeves to armhole edges. Join side and sleeve seams. Press seams.

SWEATER

MATERIALS

Lang La Paz				
Shade No. 7776 Blue Marl	12:	13:	14:	40g balls
Olympic Supra				
Shade No. 4532 Indigo Blue	3:	3:	3:	50g balls

Pair each 3mm and 4mm knitting needles.
A set of 4 × 3mm double pointed knitting needles. A cable needle.

MEASUREMENTS

To fit chest	97:	102:	107:	cm
	38:	40:	42:	in.
Actual measurements	107:	112:	117:	cm
	42:	44:	46:	in.
Length	67:	67:	69:	cm
	26¼:	26¼:	27:	in.
Sleeve length	51:	51:	51:	cm
	20:	20:	20:	in.

TENSION

20 sts and 30 rows = 10cm [4in.] over
st. st. on 4mm needles.

ABBREVIATIONS

K = knit; P = purl; st(s) = stitch(es);
st. st. = stocking stitch; rep = repeat; M1
= inc 1 st by picking up strand between
last st worked and next st, and work into
back of it; C4F [cable 4 front] = sl next
2 sts on to cable needle and hold at front,
K2, then K2 from cable needle; alt =
alternate; beg = beginning; dec =
decrease; inc = increase; cm =
centimetres; in. = inches.

BACK

With 3mm needles and blue, cast on
108(112:116) sts.
Break off blue and join in marl.
1st row. P1, K2, ★ P2, K2, rep from ★ to
last st, P1.
2nd row. K1, P2, ★ K2, P2, rep from ★ to
last st, K1.

Rep 1st and 2nd rows for 7cm [2¾in.],
ending with 2nd row.
Change to 4mm needles.
1st row. K24(25:26) sts, turn and cast on
1 st, leaving remaining sts on a spare
needle.
Continue in st. st. on these 25(26:27) sts,
starting with a P row.
Work until back measures 42(42:44)cm
[16½(16½:17¼)in.] from
commencement, ending with a P row.

Shape armhole.
Next row. Cast off 8 sts, K to end.
Continue until armhole measures 25cm
[10in.] from cast off sts, ending with a P
row.
Cast off.
Return to sts on spare needle and join in
blue.
Next row. With blue cast on 1 st, K1,
M1, K2, M1, K1, turn and cast on 1 st.
Continue on these 8 sts.
1st row [wrong side]. K2, P4, K2.
2nd row. K1, P1, K4, P1, K1.
Rep 1st and 2nd rows once more, and
then 1st row once.
6th row. K1, P1, C4F, P1, K1.

7th row. As 1st.
8th row. As 2nd.
These 8 rows form cable insertion.
Work until cable measures same as first panel ending with a wrong side row.
Cast off.
Return to sts on spare needle and join in marl, cast on 1 st, K24(25:26), turn and cast on 1 st.
Continue in st. st. on these 26(27:28) sts until 2nd panel is 5 rows less than 1st panel to shoulder, ending with a K row.

Shape back of neck.
Cast of 10 sts at beg of next row, and 5 sts at beg of 2 following alt rows.
Cast off 6(7:8) remaining sts.
Return to sts on spare needle, join in blue and work another cable over next 4 sts as 1st cable until same length as 2nd panel to back of neck.
Cast off.
Return to sts on needle and join in marl, cast on 1 st, K24(25:26), turn and cast on 1 st.
Complete 3rd panel to match 2nd panel, reversing neck shaping.
Return to sts on needle and join in blue.
Work another cable as first cable.
Return to remaining 24(25:26) sts, join in marl, cast on 1 st, K to end.
Complete to match 1st panel, having armhole shaping at opposite edge.

FRONT

Follow instructions for back until first marl panel and first cable have been completed.
Return to sts on spare needle and join in marl, cast on 1 st, K24(25:26), turn and cast on 1 st.
Continue on these 26(27:28) sts until front measures 39(39:41)cm [15½(15½:16¼)in.] from commencement, ending with a P row.

Shape neck.
Dec 1 st at end of next row, and then every 4th row until 6(7:8) sts remain.
Continue until panel measures same as first panel. Cast off.
Return to sts on needle and join in blue.
Work a cable until same length as 2nd panel to start of neck.
Cast off.
Return to sts on needle and work another panel as 2nd panel but with neck shapings at opposite edge.
Now work another cable as first cable, and then work 4th panel as first panel, but with armhole shaping at opposite edge.

SLEEVES

With 3mm needles and blue, cast on 48 sts.
Break off blue and join in marl.
Work 7cm [2¾in.] in rib as back, ending with 2nd row.

Change to 4mm needles.
1st row. K1, [M1, K4] 5 times, M1, K1, turn and cast on 1 st, leaving remaining sts on spare needle.
Continue in st. st. on these 29 sts, starting with a P row.
Work 3 rows.
Inc 1 st at beg of next row, and then every 4th row until 35 sts, and then every 6th row until 50 sts are on the needle.
Work until sleeve measures 55cm [21½in.] from commencement, ending with a P row.
Cast off loosely.
Return to sts on spare needle and join in blue.
Work a cable over next 4 sts as back until same length as first panel.
Rejoin marl to remaining sts and complete to match first panel, with side shaping at opposite edge.

MAKING UP

Join all panels.

Press each piece lightly, following instructions on ball band.
Embroider vertical lines in blue in the centre of marl panels on back and front, starting in first st above welt as picture. Work lines on sleeve in same way, the same distance on each side of centre cable. Join shoulder seams.

Neck border.
With the set of 3mm double-pointed needles and starting at right side of V-neck at edge of cable, pick up and K 220 sts evenly round neck to edge of cable on other side.
Work 2.5cm [1in.] in K2, P2 rib.
Cast off in rib with blue.
Sew side edges of neck border to centre cable, overlapping left to right.
Join side seams. Join sleeve seams leaving 4cm [1½in.] open at top.
Sew sleeves into armholes, sewing the open edges to the cast off sts.
Press seams.

CARDIGAN

MATERIALS

Lang Olympic Supra
Shade No. 4532 Indigo Blue   14:   15:   50g balls

Pair each 3mm and 4mm knitting needles. 4 buttons.

MEASUREMENTS

To fit chest	94/99:	102/107:	cm
	37/39:	40/42:	in.
Actual measurements	106:	116:	cm
	41½:	45½:	in.
Length	65:	67:	cm
	25½:	26½:	in.
Sleeve length	50:	50:	cm
	19¾:	19¾:	in.

TENSION

25 sts and 30 rows = 10cm [4in.] over patt on 4mm needles.

ABBREVIATIONS

K = knit; P = purl; st(s) = stitch(es); rep = repeat; inc = increase; patt = pattern; beg = beginning; dec = decrease; alt = alternate; sl = slip; cm = centimetres; in. = inches.

BACK

With 3mm needles cast on 125(135) sts.
1st row. K2, * P1, K1, rep from * to last st, K1.
2nd row. * K1, P1, rep from * to last st, K1.
Rep 1st and 2nd rows for 5cm [2in.], ending with 1st row.
Next row. P6(8), inc in next st, * P15(12),

inc in next st, rep from * to last 6(9) sts, P to end. [133(145) sts.]

Change to 4mm needles and patt.
1st row. * P1, K3, P5, K3, rep from * to last st, P1.
2nd and following alt rows. K all K sts and P all P sts.
3rd row. * P2, K3, P3, K3, P1, rep from * to last st, P1.
5th row. * P3, K3, P1, K3, P2, rep from * to last st, P1.
7th row. * K1, P3, K5, P3, rep from * to last st, K1.
9th row. * K2, P3, K3, P3, K1, rep from * to last st, K1.
11th row. * K3, P3, K1, P3, K2, rep from * to last st, K1.
12th row. As 2nd row.
These 12 rows form patt.
Work until back measures 40(42)cm [15¾(16½)in.] from commencement, ending with a wrong side row.

Shape armholes.
Cast off 18 sts at beg of next 2 rows.
Work until armholes measure 24cm [9½in.] from cast off sts, ending with a wrong side row.

Shape shoulders and back of neck.
Next row. Cast off 8(10) sts, patt 27(31) sts including st on needle, cast off 27 sts, patt to end.
Continue on last set of sts.
1st row. Cast off 8(10) sts, patt to end.
2nd row. Cast off 5 sts, patt to end.
Rep 1st and 2nd rows once more.
Cast off 9(11) remaining sts.
With wrong side facing, rejoin yarn to remaining sts at neck edge.
1st row. Cast off 5 sts, patt to end.
2nd row. Cast off 8(10) sts, patt to end.
3rd row. As 1st row.
Cast off 8(10) remaining sts.

RIGHT FRONT

With 3mm needles cast on 63(69) sts.

Work 5cm [2in.] in rib as back, ending with 1st row.
Next row. P to end, inc 4 sts evenly spaced. [67(73) sts.]

Change to 4mm needles and patt.

Smaller size only.
1st row. P3, K3, rep from * as 1st row on back.
2nd and following alt rows. K all K sts and P all P sts.
3rd row. P2, K3, P1, rep from * as 3rd row on back.
5th row. P1, K3, P2, rep from * as 5th row on back.
7th row. K3, P3, rep from * as 7th row on back.
9th row. K2, P3, K1, rep from * as 9th row on back.
11th row. K1, P3, K2, rep from * as 11th row on back.
12th row. As 2nd row.

Larger size only.
Work as patt on back.
Work until front measures 31(33)cm [12¼(13)in.] from commencement, ending with a wrong side row.

Shape front slope.
Dec 1 st at beg of next row, and then every 4th row until 60(66) sts remain.
Work 2 rows, ending at side edge.

Shape armhole.
Next row. Cast off 18 sts, patt to end.
Now keeping armhole edge straight, continue to dec for front slope on next and following 4th rows until 25(31) sts remain.
Work until armhole measures same as back, ending at armhole edge.

Shape shoulder.
Cast off 8(10) sts at beg of next row, and following alt row.
Work 1 row. Cast off 9(11) remaining sts.

LEFT FRONT

Follow instructions for right front, working patt rows in reverse on smaller size, and reversing shapings.
First patt row on smaller size will be:
Rep from * as 1st row on back to last 7 sts, P1, K3, P3.

SLEEVES

With 3mm needles cast on 57(57) sts.
Work 6cm [2½in.] in rib as back.
Next row. P1, inc in next st, * P4, inc in next st, rep from * to end. [69 sts.]

Change to 4mm needles and patt.
1st row. K2, P5, K3, * P1, K3, P5, K3, rep from * to last 11 sts, P1, K3, P5, K2.

Continue in patt as set.
Work 3 more rows.
Now working the new sts in patt, inc 1 st at each end of next row, and then every 4th row until 107 sts, and then every 6th row until 123 sts are on the needle.
Continue until sleeve measures 57cm [22½in.] from commencement.
Cast off.

Right side border.
With 3¾mm needles cast on 205 (213) sts.
1st row. K2, * P1, K1, rep from * to last st, K1.

2nd row. * K1, P1, rep from * to last st, K1.
Rep 1st and 2nd rows 4 times more.
Cast off in rib.

Left side border.
With 3¾mm needles cast on 205(213) sts.
Work 5 rows in rib as right side.
Next row [make buttonholes]. Rib 5, sl next 2 sts purlwise on to right-hand needle, pass first of these 2 sts over the 2nd and off the needle, sl 3rd from left-hand needle on to right-hand needle, and then sl the 2nd st over the 3rd st, rep in this way on 4th st and then sl 4th st back on to left-hand needle, turn and cast on 3 sts, * rib 23(25), make buttonhole, rep from * twice more, rib to end.
Work 4 more rows in rib.
Cast off in rib.

MAKING UP

Press each piece lightly, following instructions on ball band.
Join shoulder and side seams.
Join sleeve seams leaving 7cm [2¾in.] open at top. Sew sleeves into armholes sewing the open edges to the cast off sts at underarms.
Join the 2 pieces of border.
Place seam at centre back and sew border in position.
Press seams.
Sew on buttons.

MATERIALS

H.E.C. Aarlan Royal Tweed
Shade No. 1340 Light Green   10:   11:   12:   50g balls

Pair each 3¾mm and 4½mm knitting needles. A crochet hook. 5 buttons.

MEASUREMENTS

To fit chest	91/97:	97/102:	102/107:	cm
	36/38:	38/40:	40/42:	in.
Actual measurements	102:	107:	112:	cm
	40:	42:	44:	in.
Length	67:	68:	69:	cm
	26½:	26¾:	27:	in.
Sleeve length	48:	50:	50:	cm
	18¾:	19¾:	19¾:	in.

TENSION

20 sts and 28 rows = 10cm [4in.] over
st. st. on 4½mm needles.

ABBREVIATIONS

K = knit; P = purl; st(s) = stitch(es);
st. st. = stocking stitch; rep = repeat; inc
= increase; sl 1 = slip 1; yfwd = yarn
forward; sl 1P = slip 1 purlwise; tog =
together; alt = alternate; patt = pattern;
cm = centimetres; in. = inches; d.c. =
double crochet.

BACK

** With 3¾mm needles cast on
83(87:91) sts.
1st row. K2, * P1, K1, rep from * to
last st, K1.
2nd row. * K1, P1, rep from * to last st,
K1.
Rep 1st and 2nd rows for 7cm [2¾in.],
ending with 1st row.

Change to 4½mm needles.
Next row. P3(5:3), inc in next st, * P3, inc
in next st, rep from * to last 3(5:3) sts, P
to end. ** [103(107:113) sts.]

Continue in st. st.
Work until back measures 67(68:69)cm
[26½(26¾:27)in.] from commencement,
ending with a P row.
Cast off marking the 31st (32nd:35th) st
from each arm edge.
Centre 41(43:43) sts are for back of neck.

FRONT

Follow instructions for back from
** to **.

Continue in st. st.
Work until front measures 47(47:48)cm
[18½(18½:19)in.] from commencement,
ending with a P row.

Commence yoke.
1st row. K50(52:55) sts, yfwd, sl 1P, K1,
yfwd, sl 1P, K to end.
2nd row. P50(52:55) sts, K2 tog [the
slipped and made st],yfwd, sl 1P, K2 tog,
P to end.
3rd row. K48(50:53) sts, yfwd, sl 1P, K1,
yfwd, sl 1P, K2 tog, yfwd, sl 1P, K1,
yfwd, sl 1P, K to end.
4th row. P48(50:53) sts, [K2 tog, yfwd,
sl 1P] 3 times, K2 tog, P to end.
5th row. K46(48:51) sts, yfwd, sl 1P, K1,
[yfwd, sl 1P, K2 tog] 3 times, yfwd, sl 1P,

K1, yfwd, sl 1P, K to end.

6th row. P46(48:51) sts, [K2 tog, yfwd, sl 1P] 5 times, K2 tog, P to end.

7th row. K44(46:49) sts, yfwd, sl 1P, K1, [yfwd, sl 1P, K2 tog] 5 times, yfwd, sl 1P, K1, yfwd, sl 1P, K to end.

8th row. P44(46:49) sts, [K2 tog, yfwd, sl 1P] 7 times, K2 tog, P to end.

Continue to work 2 sts more in patt at each side, and 2 sts less in st. st. in this way on next and following alt rows until all sts are worked in patt. [**Note.** Keep extra st at each side on largest size in garter st.]

Work until front measures same as back to shoulders, ending with a wrong side row. Cast off in patt.

SLEEVES

With 3¾mm needles cast on 49(51:51) sts.

Work 6cm [2½in.] in rib as back, ending with 1st row.

Change to 4½mm needles.

Next row. P2(1:1), inc in next st, * P3, inc in next st, rep from * to last 2(1:1) sts, P2(1:1). [61(64:64) sts.]

Continue in st. st.

Work 6 rows.

Inc 1 st at each end of next row, and then every 6th row until 97(100:102) sts are on the needle.

Work until sleeve measures 48(48:50)cm [18¾(19¾:19¾)in.] from commencement, ending with a P row.

Shape top.

Cast off 7 sts at beg of next 6(4:4) rows and 8 sts at beg of 4(6:6) following rows.

Cast off 23(24:26) remaining sts.

MAKING UP

Press each piece lightly, following instructions on ball band.

Join right shoulder seam.

Neck border.

With 3¾mm needles and right side facing, pick up and K 82(86:86) sts along neck edge.

Work 19 rows in K1, P1, rib.

Cast off loosely in rib.

Fold border in half on to wrong side and slip st to picked up edge.

Work a row of d.c. along left back shoulder edge.

Now with 3¾mm needles pick up and K 39(41:45) sts evenly along front shoulder edge.

1st row. * K1, P1, rep from * to last st, K1.

2nd row. K2, * P1, K1, rep from * to last st, K1.

3rd row. As 1st row.

4th row. Rib 4, sl next 2 sts purlwise on to right-hand needle, pass first of these 2 sts over the 2nd and off the needle; sl 3rd st from left-hand needle on to right-hand needle and then pass the 2nd st over the 3rd st, then sl the 3rd st back on to left-hand needle, turn and cast on 2 sts, * rib 5(6:7) make buttonhole as before, rep from * 3 times more, rib to end.

Work 11 rows. Make buttonholes as before in next row.

Work 2 rows.

Cast off in rib.

Fold border in half on to wrong side and sl st to picked up edge.

Buttonhole st round buttonholes.

Fold border over the back at armhole edge and tack in position.

Place a marker 24(25:25.5)cm [9½(9¾:10)in.] on each side of shoulder seams to mark depth of armholes.

Join cast off edge of sleeves to armhole edges.

Join side and sleeve seams.

Press seams.

Picture opposite: **Quick To Knit** sweater in H.E.C. Aarlan Royal Tweed

BRIOCHE RIB

MATERIALS

Falkland Islands Tweed
Shade Roan   19:   20:   21:   50g balls
Pair each 3¾mm and 4mm knitting needles. 8 buttons.

MEASUREMENTS

To fit chest	97/102:	102/107:	107/112:	cm
	38/40:	40/42:	42/44:	in.
Actual measurements	112:	117:	122:	cm
	44:	46:	48:	in.
Length	63.5:	66:	67:	cm
	25:	26:	26½:	in.
Sleeve length	48:	48:	48:	cm
	19:	19:	19:	in.

TENSION

16 sts and 40 rows = 10cm [4in.] over patt on 4mm needles.

ABBREVIATIONS

K = knit; P = purl; st(s) = stitch(es); st. st. = stocking stitch; rep = repeat; patt = pattern; yfwd = yarn forward; sl 1P = slip 1 purlwise; tog = together; beg = beginning; dec = decrease; alt = alternate; inc = increase; cm = centimetres; in. = inches.

BACK

With 3¾mm needles cast on 88(92:96) sts.
1st row. P1, K2, * P2, K2, rep from * to last st, P1.
2nd row. K1, P2, * K2, P2, rep from * to last st, K1.
Rep 1st and 2nd rows 5 times more and then 1st row once, dec 1 st in centre of last row. [87(91:95) sts.]

Change to 4mm needles and patt.
1st row [wrong side]. K1, * yfwd, sl 1P, K1, rep from * to end.
2nd row. K1, * K2 tog [the slipped and made st], yfwd, sl 1P, rep from * ending K2 tog, K1.
3rd row. K1, * yfwd, sl 1P, K2 tog, rep from * ending yfwd, sl 1P, K1.
Rep 2nd and 3rd rows for patt.

Note.
The slipped and made sts which cross are always counted as 1 st.

Work until back measures 39.5(41:41)cm [15½(16:16)in.] from commencement, ending with a wrong side row.

Shape armholes.
Cast off 4(4:4) sts at beg of next 2 rows.
Dec 1 st at each end of next row, and 2 following alt rows, and then 1 st at each end of every 4th row 3(3:3) times. [67(71:75) sts.]
Work until armholes measure 22(23:24)cm [8½(9:9½)in.] measured straight, ending at armhole edge.

Shape shoulder.
Cast off at beg of next and following rows 4(3:5) sts twice, 3(4:4) sts 4 times, 4(4:4) sts twice, 3(4:4) sts twice and 4(4:4) sts twice.
Cast off 25 remaining sts for back of neck.

LEFT FRONT

** With 3¾mm needles cast on
40(42:44) sts.
1st row. P1(2:1), K2, * P2, K2, rep from
* to last 1(2:1) sts, P1(2:1).
2nd row. K1(2:1), P2, * K2, P2, rep from
* to last 1(2:1) sts, K1(2:1).
Rep 1st and 2nd rows 5 times more, and
then 1st row once, dec 1st in centre of
last row. [39(41:43) sts.]

Change to 4mm needles and patt as back.
Work 8 rows, ending with a right side
row. **

Divide for pocket.
Next row. Patt 17 sts, turn leaving
remaining sts on spare needle.

Continue on these sts.
Work 59 more rows.
Break yarn and leave sts on spare needle.
Return to sts on first spare needle.
Work 60 rows.
Continue over all the sts.
Work until front measures same as back
to armholes, ending at side edge.

Shape armhole.
Next row. Cast off 4(4:4) sts, patt to end.
Work 1 row.
Dec 1 st at beg of next row, and 2
following alt rows, and then 1 st at beg
of every 4th row 3 times.
Work 3(7:7) rows.

Shape front slope.
Dec 1 st at end of next row, and then
every 8th row until 21(23:25) sts remain.
Work until armhole measures same as
back, ending at arm edge.

Shape shoulder.
Cast off at beg of next and following alt
rows, 4(3:5) sts once, 3(4:4) sts twice,
4(4:4) sts once, and 3(4:4) sts once.
Work 1 row.
Cast off 4(4:4) remaining sts.

RIGHT FRONT

Follow instructions for left front from
** to **.

Divide for pocket.
Next row. Patt 22(24:26) sts, turn leaving
remaining sts on spare needle.
Continue on these sts.
Work 59 more rows.
Break yarn and leave sts on spare
needle.
Return to sts on first spare needle.
Work 60 rows.
Continue over all the sts.
Work until front measures same as left
front to armhole, but working 1 row
more to end at side edge.

Shape armhole.
Next row. Cast off 4(4:4) sts, patt to end.
Dec 1 st at end of next row, and 2
following alt rows, and then 1 st at end
of every 4th row 3 times.
Work 3(7:7) rows.
Complete to match left front, reversing
neck shaping and working 1 row more to
end at armhole edge before shaping
shoulder.

SLEEVES

With 3¾mm needles cast on
46(50:50) sts.
1st row. * P2, K2, rep from * to last 2 sts,
P2.
2nd row. * K2, P2, rep from * to last
2 sts, K2.
Rep 1st and 2nd rows 5 times more, and
then 1st row once, dec 1 st in centre of
last row for *1st and 2nd sizes only*, or inc
1 st in centre of last row for *3rd size only*.
[45(49:51) sts.]

**Change to 4mm needles and patt as
back.**
Work 3 rows.
Inc 1 st at each end of next row, and
then every 16th(16th:14th) row until
67(71:75) sts are on the needle.

BRIOCHE RIB

Work until sleeve measures 48cm [19in.] from commencement, ending with a wrong side row.

Shape top.
Cast off 4 sts at beg of next 2 rows.
Now dec 1 st at each end of next row, and then every alt row until 19(19:21) sts remain. Cast off.

RIGHT SIDE BORDER AND COLLAR

With 3¾mm needles cast on 156(160:164) sts.
Work 32 rows in rib as back welt.
Cast off in rib.

LEFT SIDE BORDER AND COLLAR

With 3¾mm needles cast on 156(160:164) sts.
Work in rib as right side.
Work 6 rows.
Next row [make buttonholes]. Rib 67(71:75) sts, cast off 2, * rib 25 including st on needle, cast off 2, rep from * twice more, rib to end.
Next row. Rib to end, casting on 2 sts over those cast off.
Work 16 rows.
Make buttonholes in next 2 rows as before.
Work 6 rows.
Cast off in rib.

POCKET LININGS (2)

With 4mm needles cast on 30 sts.
Work 28 rows in st. st.
Cast off.

POCKET BORDERS (2)

With 3¾mm needles cast on 34 sts.
Work 11 rows in rib as cuffs.
Cast off in rib.

MAKING UP

Press each piece lightly, following instructions on ball band.
Join shoulder, side and sleeve seams.
Sew sleeves into armholes.
Join narrow edges of collar. Place seam at centre back and sew cast on edge of borders and collar to centre front and back neck edges.
Sew pocket linings in position.
Sew cast on edge of pocket borders to pocket opening edges.
Slip st side edges in position.
Press seams.
Sew on buttons.

GIANT CABLE

MATERIALS

Berger Du Nord Lima shade 8057 Terre	9:	10:	11:	100g balls

Pair each 5½mm and 6½mm knitting needles. A cable needle.

MEASUREMENTS

To fit chest	97/102:	102/107:	107/112:	cm
	38/40:	40/42:	42/44:	in.
Actual measurements	112:	117:	122:	cm
	44:	46:	48:	in.
Length	65:	67:	69:	cm
	25½:	26¼:	27:	in.
Sleeve length	49:	51:	51:	cm
	19¼:	20:	20:	in.

TENSION

12 sts and 16 rows = 10cm [4in.] over reverse st. st. on 6½mm needles.

ABBREVIATIONS

K = knit; P = purl; st(s) = stitch(es); st. st. = stocking stitch; rep = repeat; M1 = inc 1 st by picking up strand between last st worked and next st and work into back of it; patt = pattern; C12B [cable 12 back] = slip next 6 sts on to cable needle and hold at back, K6, then K6 from cable needle; C12F [cable 12 front] = slip next 6 sts on to cable needle and hold at front, K6, then K6 from cable needle; inc = increase; dec = decrease; alt = alternate; beg = beginning; cm = centimetres; in. = inches.

FRONT

With 5½mm needles cast on 64(66:68) sts.
1st row. P1(2:1), K2, * P2, K2, rep from * to last 1(2:1) sts, P1(2:1).
2nd row. K1(2:1), P2, * K2, P2, rep from * to last 1(2:1) sts, K1(2:1).

Rep 1st and 2nd rows for 8cm [3¼in.], ending with 1st row.
Next row. Rib 3(2:3), M1, * rib 3, M1, rib 2, M1, rep from * to last 6(4:5) sts, rib 3, M1, rib 3(1:2). [88(92:94) sts.]

Change to 6½mm needles and patt.
1st row. P7(7:8), [K18, P10(12:12)] twice, K18, P7(7:8).
2nd and following alt rows. P all P sts and K all K sts.
3rd and 5th rows. As 1st row.
7th row. P7(7:8), [C12B, K6, P10(12:12)] twice, C12B, K6, P7(7:8).
9th, 11th and 13th rows. As 1st row.
15th row. P7(7:8), [K6, C12F, P10(12:12)] twice, K6, C12F, P7(7:8).
16th row. As 2nd row.
These 16 rows form the patt.
Work until front measures 60(62:64)cm [23¾(24½:25¼)in.] from commencement, ending with a wrong side row.

Shape neck.
Next row. Patt 38(39:39) sts, turn leaving remaining sts on spare needle.

Continue on these sts.
Dec 1 st at neck edge on next 7 rows, ending at armhole edge.

Shape shoulder.
Dec once more at neck edge on following alt row, and at the same time, cast off 10 sts at beg of next and following alt row at shoulder edge.
Work 1 row.
Cast off 10(10:11) remaining sts.
Rejoin yarn to remaining sts at neck edge, cast off centre 12(14:16) sts, patt to end.
Complete to match other side, working 1 row more to end at arm edge before shaping shoulder.

BACK

With 5½mm needles cast on 56(60:62) sts.
1st row. P1(1:2), K2, ★ P2, K2, rep from ★ to last 1(1:2) sts, P1(1:2).
2nd row. K1(1:2), P2, ★ K2, P2, rep from ★ to last 1(1:2) sts, K1(1:2).
Rep 1st and 2nd rows for 8cm [3¼in.], ending with 1st row.
Next row. Rib 2(4:5), M1, ★ rib 4, M1, rep from ★ to last 2(4:5) sts, rib 2(4:5). [70(74:76) sts.]

Change to 6½mm needles and reverse st. st. (P1 row, K1 row alternately.)
Work until back measures same as front to shoulders, ending with a K row.

Shape shoulders.
Cast off 8 sts at beg of next 4 rows, and 8(9:9) sts at beg of 2 following rows.
Cast off 22(24:26) remaining sts for back of neck.

SLEEVES

With 5½mm needles cast on 30(30:32) sts.
1st row. P2(2:1), K2, ★ P2, K2, rep from ★ to last 2(2:1) sts, P2(2:1).
2nd row. K2(2:1), P2, ★ K2, P2, rep from ★ to last 2(2:1) sts, K2(2:1).
Rep 1st and 2nd rows for 8cm [3¼in.] ending with 1st row.
Next row. Rib 1(1:2), M1, ★ rib 4, M1, rep from ★ to last 1(1:2) sts, rib 1(1:2). [38(38:40) sts.]

Change to 6½mm needles and reverse st. st.
Work 2 rows.
Inc 1 st at each end of next row, and then every 4th row until 68(70:72) sts are on the needle.
Work until sleeve measures 49(51:51)cm [19¼(20:20)in.] from commencement, ending with a wrong side row.
Cast off.

MAKING UP

Do not press.
Join right shoulder seam.

Neck border.
With 5½mm needles and right side facing, pick up and K 13(13:13) sts down left side of neck, 12(14:16) sts from the cast off sts, 13(13:13) sts up right side of neck, and 22(24:26) sts along back neck edge. [60(64:68) sts.]
1st row. K1, P2, ★ K2, P2, rep from ★ to last st, K1.
2nd row. P1, K2, ★ P2, K2, rep from ★ to last st, P1.
Rep 1st and 2nd rows for 4cm [1½in.].
Cast off in rib.
Join left shoulder seam.
Place a marker 28(29:30)cm [11(11½:11¾)in.] each side of shoulder seams to mark depth of armholes.
Join cast off edge of sleeves to armhole edges
Join side and sleeve seams.

MIXED PATTERNS

MATERIALS

Pingouin Confortable Sport
Shade 06 Polombe   15:   16:   17:   18: 50g balls

Pair each 3¾mm and 4½mm knitting needles. A set of 3¾mm double pointed knitting needles.

MEASUREMENTS

To fit chest	97:	102:	107:	112:	cm
	38:	40:	42:	44:	in.
Actual measurements	104:	109:	114:	119:	cm
	41:	43:	45:	47:	in.
Length	65:	65:	66:	66:	cm
	25½:	25½:	26:	26:	in.
Sleeve length	51:	51:	52:	52:	cm
	20:	20:	20½:	20½:	in.

TENSION

18 sts and 26 rows = 10cm [4in.] over patt on 4½mm needles.

ABBREVIATIONS

K = knit; P = purl; st(s) = stitch(es); rep = repeat; inc = increase; patt = pattern; 0 = no sts in this size; beg = beginning; dec = decrease; alt = alternate; cm = centimetres; in. = inches; tog = together.

BACK

With 3¾mm needles cast on 83(87:91:95) sts.
1st row. K2, * P1, K1, rep from * to last st, K1.
2nd row. *K1, P1, rep from * to last st, K1.
Rep 1st and 2nd rows for 7(7:8:8)cm [2¾(2¾:3¼:3¼)in.], ending with 2nd row.

Change to 4½mm needles.
Next row. K5(7:4:6), inc in next st, * K7(7:8:8), inc in next st, rep from * to last 5(7:5:7) sts, K to end.

[93(97:101:105) sts.]
Next row. P.

Commence patt.
1st row [right side]. P.
2nd row. P.
3rd row. K.
4th row. K.
5th row. K.
6th row. P.
7th row. P.
8th row. P1(3:5:1), K1, * P5, K1, rep from * to last 1(3:5:1) sts, P1(3:5:1).
9th row [1st and 4th sizes only]. *P3, K3, rep from * to last 3 sts, P3.
9th row [2nd size only]. K2, * P3, K3, rep from * to last 5 sts, P3, K2.
9th row [3rd size only]. P1, K3, * P3, K3, rep from * to last st, P1.
10th row [1st and 4th sizes only]. P4, K1, * P5, K1, rep from * to last 4 sts, P4.
10th row [2nd size only]. * K1, P5, rep from * to last st, K1.
10th row [3rd size only]. P2, K1, * P5, K1, rep from * to last 2 sts, P2.
11th row [1st and 4th sizes only]. * K3, P3, rep from * to last 3 sts, K3.
11th row [2nd size only]. P2, * K3, P3, rep from * to last 5 sts, K3, P2.
11th row [3rd size only]. K1, P3, * K3,

P3, rep from * to last st, K1.
Rep 8th to 11th rows 5 times more, and then 8th and 9th rows once.
34th row. P.
35th row. K.
36th row. K.
37th row. K.
38th row. P.
39th row. P.
40th row. P.
41st row. K.
42nd row. P1, * K1, P3, rep from * to end.
43rd row. K2, P1, * K3, P1, rep from * to last 2 sts, K2.
44th row. * P3, K1, rep from * to last st, P1.
45th row. * P1, K3, rep from * to last st, P1.
Work 11 more rows, moving the patt 1 st, on every row in this way.
57th row. K.
58th row. P.
59th row. P.
60th row. P.
61st row. K.
62nd row. K.
63rd row. K7(9:0:2), P2, *K9, P2, rep from * to last 7(9:0:2) sts, K7(9:0:2).
64th row. P7(9:0:2), K2, * P9, K2, rep from * to last 7(9:0:2) sts, P7(9:0:2).
65th row [1st size only]. K2, P1, K4, P2, * K4, P1, K4, P2, rep from * to last 7 sts, K4, P1, K2.
65th row [2nd size only]. *K4, P1, K4, P2, rep from * to last 9 sts, K4, P1, K4.
65th row [3rd size only]. * P2, K4, P1, K4, rep from * to last 2 sts, P2.
65th row [4th size only]. K2, * P2, K4, P1, K4, rep from * to last 4 sts, P2, K2.
66th row [1st size only]. P1, K3, P3, * K2, P3, K3, P3, rep from * to last 9 sts, K2, P3, K3, P1.
66th row [2nd size only]. P3, K3, P3, * K2, P3, K3, P3, rep from * to end.
66th row [3rd size only]. K2, * P3, K3, P3, K2, rep from * to end.
66th row [4th size only]. P2, K2, * P3, K3, P3, K2, rep from * to last 2 sts, P2.

Work 2 more rows, working 2 sts more in the diamonds on each row.
Now work 3 rows, working 2 sts less in the diamonds on each row.
72nd row. As 64th row.
73rd row. As 63rd row.
Break yarn. Slip sts from one needle to the other and with right side facing rejoin yarn and start patt again from the 1st row.
Continue until back measures 40.5cm [16in.] from commencement, ending with a wrong side row.
Cast on 2 sts at beg of next 2 rows for start of armholes.
Continue in patt, but keeping 5 sts at each side in garter st [every row K].
Work until the 2nd patt has been completed, thus ending with 73rd row.
Now K 2 rows.
Next row. K5, P27(28:29:30) and leave these sts on a st holder for left back, cast off next 33(35:37:39) sts, P to last 5 sts, K5.
Leave 32(33:34:35) sts of right back on another st holder.

FRONT

Follow instructions for back until front is 21 rows less than back to shoulders.

Shape neck.
Next row. Patt 43(44:45:46) sts, cast off 11(13:15:17) sts, patt to end.
Continue on last set of sts.
Dec 1 st at neck edge on next 8 rows, and then the 3 following alt rows.
Work 6 rows.
Leave remaining 32(33:34:35) sts on a st holder.
Rejoin yarn to remaining sts at neck edge and complete to match other side.

SLEEVES

With 3¾mm needles cast on 47(47:51:51) sts.
Work 7(7:8:8)cm [2¾(2¾:3¼:3¼)in.] in

rib as back, but ending with 1st row.

Change to 4½mm needles.
Next row. P5(5:4:4), inc in next st,
★ P4(4:5:5) inc in next st, rep from ★ to
last 6(6:4:4) sts, P to end.
[55(55:59:59) sts.]
Next row. K.
Continue in patt, starting with 36th patt
row.
Work 6 rows.
42nd patt row. P1, ★ K1, P3, rep from
★ to last 2 sts, K2.
Continue in patt as set, *at the same time*
inc 1 st at each end of next row and then
every 8th row 7 times more, and then at
each end of every 6th row 6 times,
working the extra sts in patt.
On the 63rd patt row ensure that 9
centre sts are worked K9, and after
completing this motif break yarn, slip sts
from one needle to the other and rejoin
yarn to start again on right side of work
for 1st patt row.
On the 8th patt row ensure that 5

centre sts are worked P5.
After the last inc, continue on these
83(83:87:87) sts until the 73rd row of patt
has been worked.
Now K 2 rows, and then P 3 rows.
Cast off.

MAKING UP

Press each piece lightly, following
instructions on ball band.
Graft the 2 sets of shoulder sts or if
preferred hold them tog with right sides
inside and cast off both sets tog.

Neck border.
With right-side facing and using the set
of double pointed needles, pick up and
K 92(96:100:104) sts round neck edge.
Work 5 rounds in K1, P1, rib.
Cast off in rib.
Join cast off edge of sleeves to armhole
edges.
Join side and sleeve seams.
Press seams.

3-THREAD WORKING

MATERIALS

| Wendy Pampas shade 603 Lovegrass | 15: | 15: | 18: | 18: | 50g balls |

Pair of 5½mm knitting needles.

MEASUREMENTS

To fit chest	97:	102:	107:	112:	cm
	38:	40:	42:	44:	in.
Actual measurements	107:	112:	117:	122:	cm
	42:	44:	46:	48:	in.
Length	64:	64:	65:	66:	cm
	25:	25:	25½:	26:	in.
Sleeve length	40:	40:	40:	40:	cm
	16:	16:	16:	16:	in.

TENSION

12 sts and 26 rows = 10cm [4in.] over patt on 5½mm needles using 3 strands of yarn together.

ABBREVIATIONS

K = knit; P = purl; st(s) = stitch(es); tbl = through back of loop; rep = repeat; yfwd = yarn forward; sl 1P = slip 1 purlwise; sl 1K = slip 1 knitwise; patt = pattern; tog = together; inc = increase; p.s.s.o. = pass slipped stitch over; dec = decrease; cm = centimetres; in. = inches.

FRONT

With 5½mm needles and using 3 strands of yarn together, cast on 54(56:60:62) sts.
1st row [right side]. * K1 tbl, P1, rep from * to end.
Rep this row for 6cm [2¼in.].

Commence patt.
1st row [wrong side]. K1, * K1, yfwd, sl 1P, rep from * to last st, K1.
2nd row. K1, * K2 tog [the slipped and made st], yfwd, sl 1P, rep from * to last st, K1.
Rep 2nd row only throughout for patt.

Note.
The slipped and made sts which cross are always counted as 1 st.

Work 9 more rows.
Now keeping patt correct, inc 1 st at each end of next row, and then every 14th row until 66(68:72:74) sts are on the needle.
Work until front measures 40(40:40:41)cm [15¾(15¾:15¾:16¼)in.] from commencement, ending with a wrong side row.
Mark each end of last row to indicate start of armholes.

Shape raglan armholes.
1st row. K1, K2 tog, yfwd, sl 1K, K2 tog, p.s.s.o., patt to last 5 sts, K3 tog, yfwd, sl 1P, K1.
2nd to 8th rows. Work in patt.
Rep last 8 rows 2(2:1:1) times more.
[54(56:64:66) sts.]
Continue to dec in this way at each end of next row, and then every 6th row until 30(32:32:34) sts remain.
Work 5 rows.
Cast off loosely.

BACK

Work as front.

SLEEVES

With 5½mm needles and using 3 strands of yarn together, cast on 36(36:36:36) sts. Work 6cm [2¼in.] in rib as front.

Continue in patt as front.
Work 7(7:5:5) rows.

1st and 2nd sizes only.
Keeping patt correct, inc 1 st at each end of next row, and then every 8th row until 56 sts are on the needle.

3rd and 4th sizes only.
Keeping patt correct, inc 1 st at each end of next row, and then every 6th row until 48 sts, and then every 8th row until 60 sts are on the needle.

Continue for all sizes.
Work until sleeve measures 41cm [16in.] from commencement, ending with a wrong side row.

Mark each end of last row to indicate start of sleeve top.
Shape top exactly as for front.
Cast off 20 remaining sts loosely.

MAKING UP

Press each piece lightly, following instructions on ball band.
Join front raglan seams, and right back raglan seam.

Neck border.
With 5½mm needles and using 3 strands of yarn together, pick up and K 76(78:78:82) sts evenly along neck edge.
Work 6 rows in rib.
Cast off in rib.
Join left back raglan and neck border seam.
Join side and sleeve seams.
Press seams.

COUNTRY STYLE

MATERIALS

H.E.C. Aarlan Natura
Shade No. 5301 Cream

	10:	11:	11:	100g balls

Pair each 4½mm, 5mm and 6mm knitting needles.

MEASUREMENTS

To fit chest	96/99:	99/104:	104/109:	cm
	37/39:	39/41:	41/43:	in.
Actual measurements	107:	112:	117:	cm
	42:	44:	46:	in.
Length	70:	71:	72:	cm
	27½:	28:	28¼:	in.
Sleeve length	50:	50:	50:	cm
	19¾:	19¾:	19¾:	in.

TENSION

16 sts and 20 rows = 10cm [4in.] over patt on 6mm needles.

ABBREVIATIONS

K = knit; P = purl; st(s) = stitch(es); rep = repeat; inc = increase; patt = pattern; beg = beginning; alt = alternate; dec = decrease; cm = centimetres; in. = inches.

FRONT

★★★With 5mm needles cast on 71(73:77) sts.
1st row. K2, ★ P1, K1, rep from ★ to last st, K1.
2nd row. ★ K1, P1, rep from ★ to last st, K1.
Rep 1st and 2nd rows for 9cm [3½in.], ending with 1st row.
Next row. P5(1:3), inc in next st, ★ P4, inc in next st, rep from ★ to last 5(1:3) sts, P5(1:3). [84(88:92) sts.] ★★★

Change to 6mm needles and patt.
1st row. [P1, K1] 1(2:3) times, ★ P6, [K1, P1] 4 times, K6, rep from ★ to last 2(4:6) sts, [K1, P1] 1(2:3) times.
2nd and following alt rows. K all K sts and P all P sts.
3rd row. [K1, P1] 1(2:3) times, ★ P5, [K1, P1] 5 times, K5, rep from ★ to last 2(4:6) sts, [K1, P1] 1(2:3) times.
5th row. [P1, K1] 1(2:3) times, ★ P4, [K1, P1] twice, K2, P2, [K1, P1] twice, K4, rep from ★ to last 2(4:6) sts, [K1, P1] 1(2:3) times.
7th row. [K1, P1] 1(2:3) times, ★ P3, [K1, P1] twice, K3, P3, [K1, P1] twice, K3, rep from ★ to last 2(4:6) sts, [P1, K1] 1(2:3) times.
9th row. [P1, K1] 1(2:3) times, ★ P2, [K1, P1] twice, K4, P4, [K1, P1] twice, K2, rep from ★ to last 2(4:6) sts, [K1, P1] 1(2:3) times.

11th row. [K1, P1] 1(2:3) times, ★ [P1, K1] twice, P1, K5, P5, [K1, P1] twice, K1, rep from ★ to last 2(4:6) sts, [P1, K1] 1(2:3) times.
13th row. [P1, K1] 1(2:3) times, [K1, P1] twice, K6, P6, [K1, P1] twice, rep from ★ to last 2(4:6) sts, [K1, P1] 1(2:3) times.
15th row. [K1, P1] 1(2:3) times, ★ [P1, K1] twice, P6, K6, [P1, K1] twice, rep from ★ to last 2(4:6) sts, [P1, K1] 1(2:3) times.
17th row. [P1, K1] 1(2:3) times, ★ [K1, P1] twice, K1, P5, K5, [P1, K1] twice, P1, rep from ★ to last 2(4:6) sts, [K1, P1] 1(2:3) times.
19th row. [K1, P1] 1(2:3) times, ★ K2, [P1, K1] twice, P4, K4, [P1, K1] twice, P2, rep from ★ to last 2(4:6) sts, [P1, K1] 1(2:3) times.
21st row. [P1, K1] 1(2:3) times, ★ K3, [P1, K1) twice, P3, K3, [P1, K1] twice, P3, rep from ★ to last 2(4:6) sts, [K1, P1] 1(2:3) times.
23rd row. [K1, P1] 1(2:3) times, ★ K4, [P1, K1] twice, P2, K2, [P1, K1] twice, P4, rep from ★ to last 2(4:6) sts, [P1, K1] 1(2:3) times.
25th row. [P1, K1] 1(2:3) times, ★ K5, [P1, K1] 5 times, P5, rep from ★ to last 2(4:6) sts, [K1, P1] 1(2:3) times.
27th row. [K1, P1] 1(2:3) times, ★ K6, [P1, K1) 4 times, P6, rep from ★ to last 2(4:6) sts, [P1, K1] 1(2:3) times.
28th row. As 2nd row.
These 28 rows form patt.
Work until front measures 61(62:63)cm [24(24½:25)in.] from commencement, ending with a wrong side row.

Shape neck.
Next row. Patt 38(39:41) sts, cast off 8(10:10) centre sts, patt to end.
Continue on last set of sts.
Work 1 row.
★★Cast off at beg of next and following alt rows, 3 sts once and 2 sts twice, and then dec 1 st at beg of 3 following alt rows.
Work 2 rows, ending at arm edge.

Shape shoulder.
Cast off 9(9:10) sts at beg of next row, and 9(10:10) sts at beg of following alt row.
Work 1 row.
Cast off 10(10:11) remaining sts.
Rejoin yarn to remaining sts at neck edge and follow instructions for other side from ** to end.

BACK

Follow instructions for front from *** to ***.

Change to 6mm needles and patt.
Work until back measures same as front to shoulder, ending with a wrong side row.

Shape shoulders.
Cast off at beg of next and following rows, 9(9:10) sts twice, 9(10:10) sts twice, and 10(10:11) sts twice.
Cast off 28(30:30) remaining sts.

SLEEVES

With 5mm needles cast on 39(41:41) sts.
Work 7cm [2¾in.] in rib as front, ending with 1st row.
Next row. P4(2:2), inc in next st, * P2, inc in next st, rep from * to last 4(2:2) sts, P4(2:2). [50(54:54) sts.]

Change to 6mm needles and patt.
1st row. P1(3:3), [K1, P1] 4 times, K6, * P6, [K1, P1] 4 times, K6, * P6, [K1, P1] 4 times, K1(3:3).
[Note that the 20 sts of patt rep are in centre of sleeve.]

Continue in patt as set.
Work 5 more rows.
Now working the new sts in patt, inc 1 st at each end of next row, and then every 10th row until 56(60:60) sts, and then every 6th row until 72(76:76) sts are on the needle.
Work until sleeve measures 50cm [19¾in.] from commencement, ending with a wrong side row.
Cast off loosely.

MAKING UP

Press each piece lightly, following instructions on ball band.
Join right shoulder seam.

Neck border.
With 5mm needles and right side facing, pick up and K 49(51:51) sts evenly along front neck edge, and 29(31:31) sts along back neck edge.
Work in K1, P1, rib.
Work 6 rows.

Change to 4½mm needles.
Work 8 rows.

Change to 5mm needles.
Work 3 rows.
Cast off loosely in rib.
Fold neck border in half on to wrong side and sl st loosely to picked up edge.
Place a marker 24(25:25)cm [9½(10:10)in.] on each side of shoulder seams to mark depth of armholes.
Join cast off edge of sleeves to armhole edges.
Join side and sleeve seams.
Press seams.

Picture opposite: **Country Style** sweater in H.E.C. Aarlan Natura

MATERIALS

| H.E.C. Aarlan Polo | 14: | 15: | 16: | 50g balls |

Pair each 3¼mm and 4½mm knitting needles. A cable needle.

MEASUREMENTS

To fit chest	97:	102:	107:	cm
	38:	40:	42:	in.
Actual measurements	107:	112:	117:	cm
	42:	44:	46:	in.
Length	72:	72:	74:	cm
	28¼:	28¼:	29:	in.
Sleeve length	52:	52:	52:	cm
	20½:	20½:	20½:	in.

TENSION

22 sts and 27 rows = 10cm [4in.] over st. st. on 4½mm needles.

ABBREVIATIONS

K = knit; P = purl; rep = repeat; inc = increase; st. st. = stocking stitch; patt = pattern; RT [right twist] = take the needle in front of the 1st st and K the 2nd st, then K the 1st st, slip both sts off the needle tog; LT [left twist] = take the needle behind the 1st st and K 2nd st in back loop, then K the 1st st in front loop, slip both sts off the needle tog; C3L [cross 3 left] = slip 1st st on to cable needle and leave at front, K next 2 sts, and then K st from cable needle; C3R [cross 3 right] = slip next 2 sts on to cable needle and hold at back, K next st, then K2 from cable needle; M1 = increase 1 st by picking up strand between last st worked and next st and K into back of it; C4F [cable 4 front] = slip next 2 sts on to cable needle and hold at front, K2, then K2 from cable needle; C4B [cable 4 back] = slip next 2 sts on to cable needle and hold at back, K2, then K2 from cable needle; C5F [cable 5 front] = slip next 2 sts on to cable needle and hold at front, K3, then K2 from cable needle; C5B [cable 5 back] = slip next 3 sts on to cable needle and hold at back, K2, then K3 from cable needle; tog = together; beg = beginning; dec = decrease; alt = alternate; 0 = no sts in this size; cm = centimetres; in. = inches.

BACK

With 3¼mm needles cast on 94(98:106) sts.
1st row. * P2, K2, rep from * to last 2 sts, P2.
2nd row. * K2, P2, rep from * to last 2 sts, K2.
Rep 1st and 2nd rows for 8cm [3¼in.] ending with 1st row.

Change to 4½mm needles.
Next row. P1(3:7), inc in next st, * P3, inc in next st, rep from * to last 0(2:6) sts, P0(2:6). [118(122:130 sts.]

Continue in st. st.
Work until back measures 25(25:26)cm [9¾(9¾:10¼)in.] from commencement, ending with a P row.

Commence patt.
1st row. P.
2nd row. K.
3rd row. K.

4th row. P.

Rep 1st to 4th rows twice more.

13th row. P.

14th row. K.

Rep 13th and 14th rows 3 times more.

21st row. P10(6:10), RT, * P10, RT, rep from * to last 10(6:10) sts, P10(6:10).

22nd and following alt rows. K all K sts and P all P sts.

23rd row. P10(6:10), K2, * P10, K2, rep from * to last 10(6:10) sts, P10(6:10).

24th row. As 22nd.

Rep 21st to 24th rows once more.

29th row. P9(5:9), LT, RT, * P8, LT, RT, rep from * to last 9(5:9) sts, P9(5:9).

31st row. P9(5:9), K4, * P8, K4, rep from * to last 9(5:9) sts, P9(5:9).

33rd row. P8 (4:8), C3L, C3R, * P6, C3L, C3R, rep from * to last 8(4:8) sts, P8(4:8).

35th row. P8(4:8), K6, * P6, K6, rep from * to last 8(4:8) sts, P8(4:8).

37th row. P7(3:7), C4F, M1, C4B, * P4, C4F, M1, C4B, rep from * to last 7(3:7) sts, P7(3:7).

39th row. P7(3:7), K9, * P4, K9, rep from * to last 7(3:7) sts, P7(3:7).

41st row. P6(2:6), C5F, K1, C5B, * P2, C5F, K1, C5B, rep from * to last 6(2:6) sts, P6(2:6).

43rd row. P6(2:6), K11, * P2, K11, rep from * to last 6(2:6) sts, P6(2:6).

45th row. P6(2:6), C5B, K1, C5F, * P2, C5B, K1, C5F, rep from * to last 6(2:6) sts, P6(2:6).

47th row. As 43rd row.

49th row. P7(3:7), C4B, K1, C4F, * P4, C4B, K1, C4F, rep from * to last 7(3:7) sts, P7(3:7).

50th row. K7(3:7), P4, P2 tog, P3, * K4, P4, P2 tog, P3, rep from * to last 7(3:7) sts, K7(3:7).

51st row. P7(3:7), K8, * P4, K8, rep from * to last 7(3:7) sts, P7(3:7).

53rd row. P8(4:8), C3R, C3L, * P6, C3R, C3L, rep from * to last 8(4:8) sts, P8(4:8).

55th row. As 35th row.

57th row. P9(5:9), RT, LT, * P8, RT, LT, rep from * to last 9(5:9) sts, P9(5:9).

59th row. As 31st row.

61st row. As 21st row.

63rd row. As 23rd row.

65th row. As 21st.

66th row. As 22nd row.

67th row. P.

68th row. K.

Rep 67th and 68th rows 3 times more.

75th row. K.

76th row. P.

77th row. P.

78th row. K.

Rep 75th to 78th rows twice more.

Continue in st. st.

Work until back measures 70(70:72)cm [27½(27½:28¼)in.] from commencement, ending with a P row.

Shape shoulders.

Cast off 13(14:15) sts at beg of next 4 rows, and 14(14:15) sts at beg of 2 following rows.

Cast off 38(38:40) remaining sts.

FRONT

Work as back until front is 19(21:23) rows less than back to start of shoulders, ending with a K row.

Shape neck.

Next row. P51(53:56) sts, cast off 16(16:18) sts, P to end.

Continue on last set of sts.

Dec 1 st at neck edge on the next 6 rows, and then the 5 following alt rows.

Work 2(4:6) rows, ending at armhole edge.

Shape shoulder.

Cast off 13(14:15) sts at beg of next row, and following alt row.

Work 1 row.

Cast off 14(14:15) remaining sts.

Rejoin yarn to remaining sts at neck edge and complete to match other side, working 1 row more to end at armhole edge before shaping shoulder.

SLEEVES

With 3¼mm needles cast on
54(54:58) sts.
Work 7cm [2¾in.] in rib as back, ending
with 1st row.

Change to 4½mm needles.
Next row. P1(1:3), inc in next st,
* P3(2:2), inc in next st, rep from * to last
0(1:3) sts, P0(1:3). [68(72:76) sts.]

Continue in st. st.
Work 4 rows.
Inc 1 st at each end of next row, and
then every 6th row until 104(108:112) sts
are on the needle.
Work until sleeve measures 52cm
[20½in.] from commencement, ending
with a P row.
Cast off loosely.

MAKING UP

Press each piece lightly, following
instructions on ball band.
Join right shoulder seam.

Neck border.
With 3¼mm needles and right side
facing, pick up and K 62(66:68) sts along
front neck edge, and 38(38:40) sts along
back neck edge.
1st row. K1, P2, * K2, P2, rep from * to
last st, K1.
2nd row. P1, K2, * P2, K2, rep from * to
last st, P1.
Rep 1st and 2nd rows for 4.5cm [1¾in.].
Cast off loosely in rib.
Join left shoulder and neck border seam.
Fold neck border in half on to wrong
side and slip st to picked up edge.
Place a marker 24(25.5:27)cm
[9½(10:10½)in.] on each side of shoulder
seams to mark depth of armholes.
Join cast off edge of sleeves to armhole
edges.
Join side and sleeves seams.
Press seams.

Picture opposite: **Tasteful** sweater in H.E.C.
Aarlan Polo

KNITTED IN PANELS

MATERIALS

H.E.C. Aarlan Royal Tweed
Shade No. 1325 Brown   12:   13:   13:   50g balls

Pair each 3¾mm and 4½mm knitting needles.
A set of 3¾mm double pointed knitting needles. A cable needle.

MEASUREMENTS

To fit chest	94/99:	101/104:	107/112:	cm
	37/39:	40/41:	42/44:	in.
Actual measurements	107:	113:	119:	cm
	42:	44½:	47:	in.
Length	65:	67:	68:	cm
	25½:	26¼:	26¾:	in.
Sleeve length	50:	50:	50:	cm
	19¾:	19¾:	19¾:	in.

TENSION

17½ sts and 36 rows = 10cm [4in.] over patt on 4½mm needles.

ABBREVIATIONS

K = knit; P = purl; K1B [knit one below] = insert right-hand needle into next st 1 row below and K it; st(s) = stitch(es); rep = repeat; inc = increase; patt = pattern; C6B [cable 6 back] = slip next 3 sts on to cable needle and hold at back, K3, then K3 from cable needle; beg = beginning; alt = alternate; dec = decrease; cm = centimetres; in. = inches.

FRONT

** With 3¾mm needles cast on 81(87:93) sts.
1st row. K2, * P1, K1, rep from * to last st, K1.
2nd row. * K1, P1, rep from * to last st, K1.
Rep 1st and 2nd rows for 8cm [3¼in.], ending with 2nd row.
Next row. Rib 1(4:7), inc in next st, * rib 6, inc in next st, rep from * to last 2(5:8) sts, rib to end. [93(99:105) sts.]**

Change to 4½mm needles and patt.
1st row [wrong side]. K.
2nd row. K1, * K1, K1B, rep from * to last 2 sts, K2.
3rd row. K.
4th row. K1, * K1B, K1, rep from * to end.
These 4 rows form patt.
Work until front measures 17(19:19)cm [6¾(7½:7½)in.] from commencement, ending with a right side row.
Cast off purlwise.

Make cable insertion.
With 4½mm needles cast on 10 sts.
1st row [wrong side]. K2, P6, K2.
2nd row. K1, P1, K6, P1, K1.
Rep 1st and 2nd rows once more, and then 1st row once.
6th row. K1, P1, C6B, P1, K1.
7th row. As 1st row.
8th row. As 2nd.
These 8 rows form cable insertion.
Work until the 4th row of the 19th(20th:21st) patt has been completed.
Cast off firmly.
Sew one side edge of insertion to cast off sts of front.
*** On the other side edge of insertion, pick up and K 93(99:105) sts evenly.

[5 sts for each 8 rows.]
Work 9cm [3½in.] in patt, ending with a right side row.
Cast off purlwise.
Work another cable insertion as before and sew to cast off edge. ★★★
Rep from ★★★ to ★★★ twice more.
Pick up and K 93(99:105) sts along other side edge.

Continue in patt.
Work 3 rows.

Shape neck.
Next row. Patt 41(44:47) sts, cast off 11 sts, patt to end.

Continue on last set of sts.
Work 1 row.
Cast off 3 sts at beg of next row, and 2 sts at beg of following alt row; and then dec 1 st at beg of 4(5:5) following alt rows.
Work 3 rows.
Dec 1 st at beg of next row.
Work 10 rows, ending at arm edge.

Shape shoulder.
Cast off 10(11:12) sts at beg of next row, and 10(11:12) sts at beg of following alt row.
Work 1 row.
Cast off 11(11:12) remaining sts.
Rejoin yarn to remaining sts at neck edge and complete to match other side.

BACK

Follow instructions for front from ★★ to ★★.

Change to 4½mm needles and patt [omitting cable insertions].
Work until back measures same as front to shoulders, ending with a wrong side row.

Shape shoulders.
Cast off at beg of next and following rows, 10(10:12) sts 4 times, and

10(11:12) sts twice.
Cast off 31(33:33) remaining sts.

SLEEVES

With 3¾mm needles cast on 49(51:53) sts.
Work 6cm [2½in.] in rib as front, ending with 2nd row.
Next row. Rib 4(5:5), inc in next st, ★ rib 7(7:5), inc in next st, rep from ★ to last 4(5:5) sts, rib to end. [55(57:61) sts.]

Change to 4½mm needles and patt.
Work 8 rows.
Inc 1 st at each end of next row, and then every 8th row until 87(91:95) sts are on the needle.
Continue until sleeve measures 50cm [19¾in.] from commencement, ending with a right side row.
Cast off purlwise.

MAKING UP

Press each piece lightly, following instructions on ball band.
Join shoulder seams.

Neck border.
With the set of 3¾mm double pointed needles, pick up and K 31(33:33) sts along back neck edge and 53(55:55) sts evenly along front neck edge.
Work 18 rounds in K1, P1, rib.
Cast off loosely in rib.
Fold neck border in half on to wrong side and slip st to picked up edge.
Place a marker 24.5(26:27)cm [9¾(10¼:10¾)in.] on each side of shoulder seams to mark depth of armholes.
Join cast off edge of sleeves to armhole edges.
Join side and sleeve seams. Press seams.

Picture overleaf: **Knitted In Panels** sweater in H.E.C. Aarlan Royal Tweed

KNITTED IN PANELS

2-COLOUR SLIP STITCH

MATERIALS

Avocet Tweed

Main shade 300 Trossack	9:	10:	11:	50g balls
Contrast shade 307 Cotswold	6:	6:	7:	50g balls

Pair each 3¼mm and 4mm knitting needles.

MEASUREMENTS

To fit chest	97/102:	102/107:	107/112:	cm
	38/40:	40/42:	42/44:	in.
Actual measurements	107:	113:	119:	cm
	42:	44½:	47:	in.
Length	64:	66:	69:	cm
	25:	26:	27:	in.
Sleeve length	51:	51:	52:	cm
	20:	20:	20½:	in.

TENSION

25 sts and 42 rows = 10cm [4in.] over patt on 4mm needles.

ABBREVIATIONS

K = knit; P = purl; st(s) = stitch(es); M = main; C = contrast; rep = repeat; M1 = inc 1 st by picking up strand between last st worked and next st, and work into back of it; sl 1P = slip 1 purlwise; sl 3P = slip 3 purlwise; patt = pattern; dec = decrease; alt = alternate; inc = increase; cm = centimetres; in. = inches.

FRONT

** With 3¼mm needles and M, cast on 119(125:133) sts.
1st row. K2, * P1, K1, rep from * to last st, K1.
2nd row. * K1, P1, rep from * to last st, K1.
Rep 1st and 2nd rows for 8cm [3in.], ending with 1st row.

Change to 4mm needles.

Next row. P7(3:7), M1, * P8, M1, rep from * to last 8(2:6) sts, P to end. [133(141:149) sts.]
Join in C.

Commence patt.
1st row. With C: K5, * sl 3P with yarn at back, K5, rep from * to end.
2nd row. With C: K2, P1, K2, * sl 3P with yarn at front, K2, P1, K2, rep from * to end.
3rd row. With M: K2, * sl 1P with yarn at back, K7, rep from * to last 3 sts, sl 1P, K2.
4th row. With M: K1, P1, * sl 1P with yarn at front, P7, rep from * to last 3 sts, sl 1P, P1, K1.
5th row. As 1st row.
6th row. As 2nd row.
7th row. As 3rd row.
8th row. With M: K1, P to last st, K1.
9th row. With C: K1, * sl 3P with yarn at back, K5, rep from * to last 4 sts, sl 3P, K1.
10th row. With C: K1, * sl 3P with yarn at front, K2, P1, K2, rep from * to last 4 sts, sl 3P, K1.

11th row. With M: K6, ★ sl 1P with yarn at back, K7, rep from ★ to last 7 sts, sl 1P, K6.

12th row. With M: K1, P5, ★ sl 1P with yarn at front, P7, rep from ★ to last 7 sts, sl 1P, P5, K1.

13th row. As 9th row.

14th row. As 10th row.

15th row. As 11th row.

16th row. As 8th row.

These 16 rows form the patt.★★

Work until front measures 56(58:60)cm [22(23:23½)in.] from commencement, ending with a wrong side row.

Shape neck.

Next row. Patt 58(62:66) sts, turn leaving remaining sts on spare needle.

Continue on these sts.

Dec 1 st at neck edge on next 8 rows, and then the 6(6:7) following alt rows.

Work 13 rows without shaping.

Cast off 44(48:51) remaining sts.

Rejoin yarn to remaining sts at neck edge, cast off 17 centre sts, patt to end.

Complete to match other side.

BACK

Follow instructions for front from ★★ to ★★.

Work until back is 6 rows less than front to shoulders.

Shape back of neck.

Next row. Patt 49(53:56) sts, turn leaving remaining sts on spare needle.

Continue on these sts.

Dec 1 st at neck edge on next 5 rows.

Cast off 44(48:51) remaining sts.

Rejoin yarn to remaining sts at neck edge, cast off 35(35:37) centre sts, patt to end.

Complete to match other side.

SLEEVES

With 3¼mm needles and M, cast on 55(55:55) sts, and work 8cm [3in.] in rib as front, ending with 1st row.

Change to 4mm needles.

Next row. P1, M1, ★ P4, M1, rep from ★ to last 2 sts, P2. [69 sts.]

Commence patt.

Work 4 rows.

Now working the new sts in patt, inc 1 st at each end of next row, and then every 4th row until 103(103:111) sts, and then every 6th row until 137(137:141) sts are on the needle.

Work until sleeve measures 51(51:52)cm [20(20:20½)in.] from commencement, ending with a wrong side row.

Cast off.

MAKING UP

Press each piece lightly, following instructions on ball band.

Join right shoulder seam.

Neck border.

With 3¼mm needles and M, pick up and K 29(29:30) sts down left side of front neck edge, 17 sts from the cast off sts, 28(28:29) sts up right side of neck, and 45(45:47) sts along back neck edge.

Work 11 rows in rib as welt, starting with 2nd row.

Cast off in rib.

Join left shoulder and neck border seam.

Place a marker 28(28:29)cm [11(11:11½)in.] on each side of shoulder seams to mark depth of armholes.

Join cast off edge of sleeves to armhole edges.

Join side and sleeve seams. Press seams.

For illustration of **2-Colour Slip Stitch** sweater, see page 53

QUICK BRIOCHE RIB

MATERIALS

H.E.C. Aarlan Royal Tweed

Shade No. 1329 Brown	12:	13:	13:	14:	50g balls

Pair each 3¾mm and 5mm knitting needles. 4 buttons.

MEASUREMENTS

To fit chest	97:	102:	107:	112:	cm
	38:	40:	42:	44:	in.
Actual measurements	107:	112:	117:	122:	cm
	42:	44:	46:	48:	in.
Length	68:	68:	70:	70:	cm
	26¾:	26¾:	27½:	27½:	in.
Sleeve length	49:	49:	49:	49:	cm
	19¼:	19¼:	19¼:	19¼:	in.

TENSION

16 sts and 36 rows = 10cm [4in.] over patt on 5mm needles.

ABBREVIATIONS

K = knit; P = purl; st(s) = stitch(es); rep = repeat; inc = increase; patt = pattern; yfwd = yarn forward; sl = slip; sl 1P = slip 1 purlwise; tog = together; dec = decrease; beg = beginning; alt = alternate; cm = centimetres; in. = inches.

FRONT

★★ With 3¾mm needles cast on 78(82:86:90) sts.
1st row. ★ P2, K2, rep from ★ to last 2 sts, P2.
2nd row. ★ K2, P2, rep from ★ to last 2 sts, K2.
Rep 1st and 2nd rows for 11cm [4¼in.] ending with 1st row, and inc 5 sts evenly spaced in last row. [83(87:91:95) sts.]★★

Change to 5mm needles and patt.
1st row [wrong side]. K1, ★ yfwd, sl 1P, K1, rep from ★ to end.
2nd row. K1, ★ K2 tog [the slipped and made st], yfwd, sl 1P, rep from ★ ending K2 tog, K1.
3rd row. K1, ★ yfwd, sl 1P, K2 tog, rep from ★ ending yfwd, sl 1P, K1.
Rep 2nd and 3rd rows for patt.

Note.
The slipped and made sts which cross are always counted as 1 st.

Work until front measures 38(38:40:40)cm [15(15:15¾:15¾)in.] from commencement, ending with a right side row.

Divide for front opening.
Next row. Patt 39(41:43:45) sts, cast off 5 sts, patt to end.

Continue on last set of sts.
Work 14(14:12:12) rows, ending at side edge.

Shape armhole.
Next row. Cast off 3 sts, patt to end.
Work 1 row.
Dec 1 st at beg of next row, and then every alt row until 32(33:34:35) sts remain.
Work 54(52:52:50) rows, ending at opening edge.

Shape neck.
Next row. Cast off 4 sts, patt to end.
Work 1 row.

Dec 1 st at beg of next row, and then every alt row until 24(25:25:26) sts remain, and then every 4th row until

21(22:22:23) sts remain.
Work 8 rows.
Cast off.
With right side facing, rejoin yarn to remaining sts at opening edge.
Work 15(15:13:13) rows, ending at side edge.

Shape armhole.

Next row. Cast off 3 sts, patt to end.
Dec 1 st at end of next row, and then every alt row until 32(33:34:35) sts remain.
Work 54(52:52:50) rows, ending at armhole edge.

Shape neck.

Next row. Patt to last 4 sts, cast off these sts. Break yarn.
Turn and rejoin yarn to remaining sts and complete to match other side, reversing shapings.

BACK

Follow instructions for front from ** to **.

Change to 5mm needles and patt.

Work until back measures same as front to armholes, ending with a wrong side row.

Shape armholes.

Cast off 3 sts at beg of next 2 rows.
Now dec 1 st at each end of next row, and then every alt row until 69(71:73:75) sts remain.
Work until armholes are 4 rows less than front to shoulders, ending with a wrong side row.

Shape back of neck.

Next row. Patt 24(25:25:26) sts, cast off 21(21:23:23) sts, patt to end.

Continue on last set of sts.

Dec 1 st at neck edge on next 3 rows.
Cast off 21(22:22:23) remaining sts.

With wrong side facing, rejoin yarn to remaining sts at neck edge and complete to match other side.

SLEEVES

With 3¾mm needles cast on 40(40:42:42) sts.
1st row. P1(1:2:2), K2, ★ P2, K2, rep from ★ to last 1(1:2:2) sts, P1(1:2:2).
2nd row. K1(1:2:2), P2, ★ K2, P2, rep from ★ to last 1(1:2:2) sts, K1(1:2:2).
Rep 1st and 2nd rows for 7cm [2¾in.], ending with 1st row.
Next row. Rib 3(3:4:4), inc in next st, ★ rib 7, inc in next st, rep from ★ to last 4(4:5:5) sts, rib to end. [45(45:47:47) sts.]

Change to 5mm needles and patt.

Work 5 rows.
Now working the new sts in patt, inc 1 st at each end of next row, and then every 6th row until 59(59:61:61) sts, and then every 8th row until 83(83:85:85) sts are on the needle.
Work until sleeve measures 49cm [19¼in.] from commencement, ending with a wrong side row.

Shape top.

Cast off 3 sts at beg of next 2 rows.
Now dec 1 st at each end of every row until 21 sts remain.
Cast off, dec at each end of row.

MAKING UP

Press each piece lightly, following instructions on ball band.
Join shoulder seams.

Neck border.

With 3¾mm needles and right side facing, pick up and K 23(23:24:24) sts along right front neck edge, 34(34:36:36) sts evenly along back neck edge, and 23(23:24:24) sts along left front neck edge.
1st row. K1, P2, ★ K2, P2, rep from ★ to last st, K1.

2nd row. P1, K2, ★ P2, K2, rep from ★ to last st, P1.
Rep 1st and 2nd rows 9 times more, and then 1st row once.
Cast off in rib.
Fold neck border in half on to wrong side and slip st to picked up edge.

Button border.
Starting at cast off sts, pick up and K 58 sts evenly along opening edge to folded edge of neck border (approx 2 sts for each 3 rows).
1st row. ★ K2, P2, rep from ★ to last 2 sts, K2.
2nd row. ★ P2, K2, rep from ★ to last 2 sts, P2.
Rep 1st and 2nd rows 4 times more, and then 1st row once.
Cast off in rib.

Buttonhole border.
Starting at folded edge of border, pick up and K sts as button border.
Work 5 rows in rib.
Next row [make buttonholes]. Rib 4, sl next 2 sts purlwise on to right-hand needle, pass first of these 2 sts over the 2nd and off the needle; sl 3rd st from left-hand needle on to right-hand needle, and then pass the 2nd st over the 3rd st, then sl the 3rd st back on to left-hand needle, turn and cast on 2 sts; ★ rib 11, make buttonhole as before, rep from ★ twice more, rib to end.
Work 5 more rows in rib.
Cast off in rib.
Join side edges of border to cast off sts at centre front, overlapping left side over right side.
Join side and sleeve seams.
Sew sleeves into armholes.
Press seams.
Sew on buttons.

COLOUR PLAY

MATERIALS

H.E.C. Aarlan Royal

Shade No. 4236 Blue	3:	3:	40g balls
Shade No. 4239 Grey	3:	3:	40g balls
Shade No. 4285 Turquoise	2:	2:	40g balls
Shade No. 4286 Blue Green	3:	3:	40g balls
Shade No. 4237 Green	2:	2:	40g balls
Shade No. 4245 Light Blue	2:	2:	40g balls

Pair each 3¼mm and 4mm knitting needles.

MEASUREMENTS

To fit chest	91/97:	97/102:	cm
	36/38:	38/40:	in.
Actual measurements	107:	112:	cm
	42:	44:	in.
Length	66:	66:	cm
	26:	26:	in.
Sleeve length	50:	50:	cm
	19¾:	19¾:	in.

TENSION

21 sts and 27 rows = 10cm [4in.] over patt on 4mm needles.

ABBREVIATIONS

K = knit; P = purl; st(s) = stitch(es); st. st. = stocking stitch; inc = increase; rep = repeat; beg = beginning; alt = alternate; dec = decrease; tog = together; cm = centimetres; in. = inches.

Note.

Ensure that yarns are twisted together on the wrong side when changing colour to avoid holes.

FRONT

With 3¼mm needles and grey, cast on 94(100) sts.
Work 8cm [3¼in.] in K1, P1, rib.
Next row. Rib 4(7), inc in next st, * rib 4, inc in next st, rep from * to last 4(7) sts, rib to end. [112(118) sts.]
Change to 4mm needles and st. st., working colour patt as follows:
1st row. K: 83(86) blue; 29(32) turquoise.
2nd and following alt rows. P: working in same colours as previous row.
Work 22 more rows, working 1 st less in blue and 1 st more in turquoise on every K row.
Next row. K: 44(47) blue green; 68(71) light blue.
Following row. As 2nd row.
Work 12 more rows, working 1 st less in blue green and 1 st more in light blue on every K row.
Next row. K: 84(90) green; 28(28) grey.
Following row. As 2nd row.
Work 16 more rows, working 1 st more in green and 1 st less in grey on every K row.
Next row. K: 50(53) blue green; 62(65) blue.
Following row. As 2nd row.
Work 24 more rows, working 1 st more in blue green, and 1 st less in blue on every K row.

Next row. K: 27(27) turquoise; and the rest in light blue.
Following row. As 2nd row.
Work 16 more rows, working 1 st more in turquoise and 1 st less in light blue on every K row.
Next row. K: 84(88) blue; and the rest in green.
Following row. As 2nd row.
Work 12 more rows, working 1 st less in blue and 1 st more in green on every K row.
Next row. K: 40(41) light blue; 44(48) grey; and the rest in turquoise.
Following row. As 2nd row.
Work 24 more rows, working 1 st less in light blue and turquoise, and 2 sts more in grey on every K row, and *at the same time* on the 17th row in grey shape neck as follows:
K51(53) sts, cast off 10(12) sts, K to end.
Continue on last set of sts.
Work 1 row.
Cast off at beg of next and following alt rows, 3 sts once and 2 sts twice, and then dec 1 st at beg of following alt row.
Work 1 row.
Now work 13 rows in blue green, *at the same time* dec 1 st at beg of next row and 3 following alt rows, and then 1 st at beg of following 4th row.

Shape shoulder.
Cast off 12(14) sts at beg of next row, and 13 sts at beg of following alt row.
Work 1 row.
Cast off 13 remaining sts.
With wrong side facing, rejoin yarn to remaining sts at neck edge. Continuing to work 1 st more in grey and 1 st less in light blue on every K row, cast off at beg of next and following alt rows, 3 sts once and 2 sts twice, and then dec 1 st at beg of 2 following alt rows.
Next row. K: 14(15) turquoise, and the rest in blue green.
Following row. P2 tog, P to end, working in same colours as previous row.

Now working 1 st more in turquoise, and 1 st less in blue green on every K row, work 10 more rows, and at the same time, dec 1 st at beg of 2 following alt rows, and then the following 4th row.
Shape shoulder as other side.

BACK

Work as front up to start of shoulders, but omitting neck shaping.

Shape shoulders.
Cast off 12(14) sts at beg of next 2 rows,

and 13 sts at beg of 4 following rows.
Cast off remaining 36(38) sts loosely.

SLEEVES

With 3¼mm needles and grey, cast on
48(50) sts.
Work 7cm [2¾in.] in K1, P1, rib.
Next row [1st size only]. ★ Rib 2, inc in
next st, rep from ★ to end.
Next row [2nd size only]. Inc in first
2 sts, ★ rib 2, inc in next st, rep from ★ to
end. [64(68) sts.]
Change to 4mm needles and st. st.,
working in colour patt as follows:
1st row. K: 12 blue, and the remainder in
turquoise.
2nd and following alt rows. P: working
in same colour as previous row.
Work 18 more rows working 1 st more in
blue and 1 st less in turquoise on every K
row, and at the same time inc 1 st at each
end of 7th row and following 6th rows.
Continue to inc 1 st at each end of 6th
row from previous inc, and following
6th rows, and *at the same time* continue
colour patt as follows:
Next row. With blue green, K over the
sts in blue and 11 sts of the turquoise;
with light blue, K to end.
Following row. As 2nd row.
Work 12 more rows working 1 st more in
blue green and 1 st less in light blue on
every K row.
Next row. With green, K13; with grey,
K to end.
Following row. As 2nd row.
Work 18 more rows working 1 st more in
green, and 1 st less in grey on every
K row.
Next row. With blue green, inc in 1st st,
K over the sts in green, and 37 sts of the

grey; with blue K to last st, inc in last st.
Following row. As 2nd row.
Work 24 more rows, working 1 st less in
blue green, and 1 st more in blue on
every K row.
Next row. With turquoise, K39; with
light blue, K to end.
Following row. As 2nd row.
Work 14 more rows, working 1 st less in
turquoise and 1 st more in light blue on
every K row.
Next row. With blue, inc in 1st st, K over
the turquoise sts and 16 sts of the light
blue; with grey, K to last st, inc in last st.
Following row. As 2nd row.
Continue working 1 st more in blue, and
1 st less in grey on every K row until
sleeve measures 50cm [19¾in.] from
commencement, at the same time inc 1 st
at each end of 4th row from previous
inc, and 2 following 4th rows.
Cast off the 102(106) sts.

MAKING UP

Press each piece lightly, following
instructions on ball band.
Joint right shoulder seam.

Neck border.
With 3¼mm needles and grey, pick up
and K 60(62) sts along front neck edge,
and 34(36) sts along back neck edge.
Work 9 rows in K1, P1, rib.
Cast off in rib.
Join left shoulder and neck border seam.
Place a marker 25(26)cm [10(10¼)in.] on
each side of shoulder seams to mark
depth of armholes.
Join cast-off edge of sleeves to armhole
edges.
Join side and sleeve seams. Press seams.

MATERIALS

H.E.C. Aarlan Arwetta

Shade No. 104 Cream	8:	8:	9:	50g balls
Shade No. 3 Light Grey	5:	6:	6:	50g balls
Shade No. 4 Grey	5:	5:	6:	50g balls
Shade No. 5 Dark Grey	2:	3:	3:	50g balls

Pair each 3¾mm and 4½mm knitting needles. A set of 3¾mm and 4½mm double pointed knitting needles.

MEASUREMENTS

To fit chest	91/97:	97/102:	102/107:	cm
	36/38:	38/40:	40/42:	in.
Actual measurements	102:	107:	112:	cm
	42:	44:	46:	in.
Length	69:	71:	71:	cm
	27½:	28:	28:	in.
Sleeve length to shoulder	52½:	52½:	52½:	cm
	20¾:	20¾:	20¾:	in.

TENSION

19 sts and 42 rows = 10cm [4in.] over patt on 4½mm needles.

ABBREVIATIONS

K = knit; P = purl; st(s) = stitch(es); rep = repeat; inc = increase; patt = pattern; sl 1P = slip 1 purlwise; yfwd = yarn forward; tog = together; beg = beginning; dec = decrease; alt = alternate; 0 = no sts in this size; cm = centimetres; in. = inches.

BACK

With 3¾mm needles and using 1 strand each of dark grey and grey, cast on 85(89:93) sts.
1st row. K2, * P1, K1, rep from * to last st, K1.
2nd row. * K1, P1, rep from * to last st, K1.
Rep 1st and 2nd rows for 7cm [2¾in.], ending with 2nd row.
Next row. Rib 4(6:4), inc in next st, * rib 3, inc in next st, rep from * to last 4(6:4) sts, rib to end. [105(109:115) sts.]

Change to 4½mm needles and patt.
1st row [wrong side]. K1, * yfwd, sl 1P, K1, rep from * to end.
2nd row. K1, * K2 tog [the slipped and made st], yfwd, sl 1P, rep from * ending K2 tog, K1.
3rd row. K1, * yfwd, sl 1P, K2 tog, rep from * ending yfwd, sl 1P, K1.
Rep 2nd and 3rd rows for patt.

Note.
The slipped and made sts which cross are always counted as 1 st.

Continue until back measures 17(17:17.5)cm [6¾(6¾:7)in.] from commencement, ending with a wrong side row.
Now work 17(17:17.5)cm [6¾(6¾:7)in.] using 1 strand each of grey and light grey.
Now using 1 strand each of light grey and cream work 10(11:9.5)cm

[4(4¼:3¾)in.] ending with a wrong side row.

Shape armholes.
Cast off 5(5:6) sts at beg of next 2 rows.
Work until last stripe measures 17(17:17.5)cm [6¾(6¾:7)in.] ending with a wrong side row.
Continue using 2 strands of cream.
Work until armholes measure 23(24:24.5)cm [9(9½:9¾)in.] from cast off sts, ending with a wrong side row.

Shape shoulders.
Cast off 15(15:16) sts at beg of next 2 rows, and 15(16:16) sts at beg of 2 following rows.
Cast off 35(37:39) remaining sts.

FRONT

Follow instructions for back until front is 29 rows less than back to start of shoulders, ending with a right side row.

Shape neck.
Next row. Patt 41(42:44) sts, cast off 13(15:15) sts, patt to end.

Continue on last set of sts.
Dec 1 st at neck edge on next 5 rows, and then the 6(6:7) following alt rows.
Work until armhole measures same as back, ending at armhole edge.

Shape shoulder.
Cast off 15(15:16) sts at beg of next row.
Work 1 row.
Cast off 15(16:16) remaining sts.
Rejoin yarn to remaining sts at neck edge, and complete to match other side, working 1 row more to end at armhole edge before shaping shoulder.

SLEEVES

With 3¾mm needles cast on 47(47:49) sts.
Work 7cm [2¾in.] in rib as back, ending with 2nd row.
Next row. Rib 4(1:2), inc in next st, ★ rib 2, inc in next st, rep from ★ to last 3(0:1) sts, rib 3(0:1). [61(63:65) sts.]
Change to 4½mm needles and continue in patt and stripes as back.
Work 10 rows.
Now working the new sts in patt, inc 1 st at each end of next row, and then every 12th row until 89(91:93) sts are on the needle.
Work until sleeve measures 52.5cm [20¾in.] from commencement.
Cast off.

MAKING UP

Press each piece lightly, following instructions on ball band.
Join shoulder seams.

Collar.
Using the set of 3¾mm double pointed needles, pick up and K 35(37:39) sts along back neck edge, and 69(73:73) sts evenly along front neck edge.
Work 8cm [3in.] in rounds of K1, P1, rib.
Change to the set of 4½mm needles and work 10cm [4in.], and then with the set of 3¾mm needles work 6cm [2½in.] in K1, P1, rib.
Cast off loosely in rib.
Join side seams.
Join sleeve seams leaving 2.5(2.5:3)cm [1(1:1¼)in.] open at top.
Sew in sleeves, sewing the open edges to the cast off sts at underarms.
Press seams.

Picture opposite: **Neo-Classic** sweater in H.E.C. Aarlan Arwetta

CHESSBOARD

MATERIALS

Patons Moorland D.K. shade 6520 Cream	3:	4:	50g balls
Patons Baby Cotton D.K. shade 6250 Cotton Cream	3:	3:	50g balls
Patons Mohair Focus shade 2030 Ivory	10:	12:	25g balls

Pair each 3¾mm and 5mm knitting needles.

MEASUREMENTS

To fit chest	97/102:	107/112:	cm
	38/40:	42/44:	in.
Actual measurements	107:	117:	cm
	42:	46:	in.
Length	65:	70:	cm
	25½:	27½:	in.
Sleeve length	48:	50:	cm
	19:	19½:	in.

TENSION

16 sts and 22 rows = 10cm [4in.] over st. st.
1 patt square measures approx 10(11)cm [4(4½)in.] on 5mm needles.

ABBREVIATIONS

K = knit; P = purl; st(s) = stitches; A = Moorland D.K.; B = Mohair Focus; C = Baby Cotton D.K.; rep = repeat; tog = together; patt = pattern; K1B [K1 below] = insert right-hand needle into next st 1 row below and K it; st. st. = stocking stitch; inc = increase; cm = centimetres; in. = inches.

FRONT

With 3¾mm needles and A, cast on 94(106) sts.
1st row. * P2, K2, rep from * to last 2 sts, P2.
2nd row. * K2, P2, rep from * to last 2 sts, K2.
Rep 1st and 2nd rows 5 times more, and then 1st row once.
Next row. Rib 8(4), K2 tog, * rib 10, K2 tog, rep from * to last 12(4) sts, rib to end. [87(97) sts.] Break off A.

Change to 5mm needles and patt.
Instructions given for smaller size. For larger size work 2 more sts and 2 more rows in each square.
1st row. With B, K18; with C, [P1, K1] 8 times, P1; with A, [K1, P1] 8 times, K1; with B, K17; with C, [P1, K1] 9 times.
2nd row. With C, [K1, P1] 9 times; with B, K17; with A, [P1, K1B] 8 times, P1; with C, [P1, K1] 8 times, P1; with B, K18.
3rd row. With B, K18; with C, [P1, K1] 8 times, P1; with A, [K1B, P1] 8 times, K1B; with B, K17; with C, [P1, K1] 9 times.
Rep 2nd and 3rd rows 14 times more, and then 2nd row once.
33rd row. With C, [K1, P1] 9 times; with A, [K1, P1] 8 times, K1; with B, K17; with C, [P1, K1] 8 times, P1; with A, [K1, P1] 8 times, K2.
34th row. With A, K1, [P1, K1B] 8 times, P1; with C, [P1, K1] 8 times, P1; with B, K17; with A, [P1, K1B] 8 times, P1; with C, [P1, K1] 9 times.
35th row. With C, [K1, P1] 9 times; with A, [K1B, P1] 8 times, K1B, with B, K17;

with C, [P1, K1] 8 times, P1; with A,
[K1B, P1] 8 times, K1B, K1.
Rep 34th and 35th rows 14 times more
and then 34th row once.
65th row. With A, K2, [P1, K1] 8 times;
with B, K17; with C, [P1, K1] 8 times, P1;
with A, [K1, P1] 8 times, K1; with B,
K18.
66th row. With B, K18; with A, [P1, K1B]
8 times, P1; with C, [P1, K1] 8 times, P1;
with B, K17; with A, [P1, K1B] 8 times,
P1, K1.
67th row. With A, K1, K1B, [P1, K1B] 8
times; with B, K17; with C, [P1, K1] 8
times, P1; with A, [K1B, P1] 8 times,
K1B; with B, K18.
Rep 66th and 67th rows 14 times more,
and then 66th row once.
These 96(102) rows form the patt.
Rep them once more.
Cast off loosely in patt.

Neck border.
With right side facing and A, and using
3¾mm needles pick up and K 1 st from
each of the centre 41(43) cast off sts.
1st row. * K1, P1, rep from * to last st,
K1.
2nd row. K1, * K1B, P1, rep from * to
last 2 sts, K1B, K1.
3rd row. K1, * P1, K1B, rep from * to last
2 sts, P1, K1.
Rep 2nd and 3rd rows 11 tims more.
Cast off in patt.

BACK

Work as front.

SLEEVES

With 3¾mm needles and A, cast on
50(54) sts.
Work 16 rows in rib as front. Break off A.

Change to 5mm needles.
Join in B and continue in reverse st. st.
[P1 row, K1 row alternately.]
Work 4 rows.
Inc 1 st at each end of next row, and
then every 4th row until 92(98) sts are on
the needle.
Work until sleeve measures 48(50)cm
[19(19½)in.] from commencement,
ending with a P row.
Cast off loosely knitwise.

MAKING UP

Do not press.
Join shoulder and neck border seams.
Fold border in half on to wrong side and
slip st to picked up edge.
Place a marker 29(30.5)cm [11½(12)in.]
on each side of shoulder seams to mark
depth of armholes.
Join cast off edge of sleeves to armhole
edges.
Join side and sleeve seams.

Picture overleaf: **Chessboard** sweater in
Patons wools

CHESSBOARD

NORWEGIAN TECHNIQUE

MATERIALS

Patons Beehive D.K. with Mountain Wool

Main shade 6345 Bedale	7:	7:	8:	8:	50g balls
1st contrast shade 6356 Wharfedale	3:	4:	4:	4:	50g balls
2nd contrast shade 6340 Wensleydale	1:	1:	1:	1:	50g ball

Pair each 3¼mm and 4mm knitting needles.

MEASUREMENTS

To fit chest	94:	99:	104:	109:	cm
	37:	39:	41:	43:	in.
Actual measurements	104:	109:	113:	117:	cm
	41:	43:	44½:	46:	in.
Length	63.5:	66:	68.5:	70:	cm
	25:	26:	27:	27½:	in.
Sleeve length	48:	48:	49.5:	49.5:	cm
	19:	19:	19½:	19½:	in.

TENSION

24 sts and 28 rows = 10cm [4in.] over patt on 4mm needles.

ABBREVIATIONS

K = knit; P = purl; st(s) = stitch(es); st. st. = stocking stitch; rep = repeat; M = main; A = 1st contrast; B = 2nd contrast; M1 = increase 1 st by picking up strand between last st worked and next st, and work into back of it; patt = pattern; dec = decrease; inc = increase; sl 1 = slip 1; cm = centimetres; in. = inches.

FRONT

** With 3¼mm needles and M, cast on 108(112:116:120) sts.
1st row. P1, K2, * P2, K2, rep from * to last st, P1.
2nd row. K1, P2, * K2, P2, rep from * to last st, K1.
Rep 1st and 2nd rows for 8cm [3in.], ending with 1st row.
Next row. Rib 6(5:4:3), M1, * rib 6, M1, rep from * to last 6(5:4:3) sts, rib to end. [125(130:135:140) sts.]

Change to 4mm needles and patt.

Note. Strand yarn not in use loosely across back of work to keep fabric elastic.

1st to 4th rows. With M, work in st. st., starting with a K row.
5th row. K: * 1M, 3A, 1M, rep from * to end.
6th row. P: * 1M, 3A, 1M, rep from * to end.
7th to 10th rows. Rep 5th and 6th rows twice.
11th row. K: * 1B, 3M, 1B, rep from * to end.
12th row. P: * 1B, 3M, 1B, rep from * to end.
13th to 18th rows. As 5th to 10th rows.
19th to 22nd rows. As 1st to 4th rows.
These 22 rows form the patt. **
Work until front measures 46(48.5:51:51)cm [18(19:20:20)in.] from commencement, ending with a wrong side row.

Divide for neck.
Next row. K62(65:67:70) sts, turn leaving remaining sts on spare needle.

Continue on these sts.
Work 1 row.
Dec 1 st at neck edge on next row, and then every alt row until 39(41:43:45) sts remain.
Work 1 row.
Cast off.
With right side facing, rejoin yarn to remaining sts at neck edge.
1st and 3rd sizes only. Cast off 1 st, K to end.
2nd and 4th sizes only. K to end.
Complete to match other side, reversing shaping.

BACK

Follow instructions for front from ** to **.
Continue until back measures same as front to shoulders, ending with a wrong side row.
Cast off marking the 37th(39th:41st:43rd) st from each arm edge.
Centre 51(52:53:54) sts are for back of neck.

SLEEVES

With 3¼mm needles and M, cast on 54(54:58:58) sts.
1st row. * P2, K2, rep from * to last 2 sts, P2.
2nd row. * K2, P2, rep from * to last 2 sts, K2.
Rep 1st and 2nd rows for 8cm [3in.], ending with 1st row.
Next row. Rib 2(2:1:1), M1, * rib 5, M1, rep from * to last 2 sts, rib 2.
[65(65:70:70) sts.]

Change to 4mm needles and patt as front.
Work 4 rows.

Now working the new sts in patt, inc 1 st at each end of next row, and then every 4th row until 115(115:122:122) sts are on the needle.
Work until sleeve measures 48(48:49.5:49.5)cm [19(19:19½:19½)in.] from commencement, ending with a wrong side row.
Cast off loosely.

COLLAR

With 3¼mm needles and M, cast on 148(148:152:152) sts.
1st row. P1, K2, * P2, K2, rep from * to last st, P1.
2nd row. K1, * P2, K2, rep from * to last st, K1.
Rep 1st and 2nd rows 6 times more.
Continue as follows:
1st row. Rib to last 6 sts, turn.
2nd row. Sl 1, rib to last 6 sts, turn.
3rd row. Sl 1, rib to last 8 sts, turn.
4th row. As 3rd row.
5th row. Sl 1, rib to last 10 sts, turn.
6th row. As 5th row.
Continue to work 2 sts less on every row in this way until 18 sts are left unworked at each end of the needle.
Next row. Sl 1, rib to end.
Work 1 row in rib.
Cast off loosely in rib.

MAKING UP

Join shoulder seams.
Place a marker 25.5(25.5:27:27)cm [10(10:10½:10½)in.] on each side of shoulder seams to mark depth of armholes.
Join cast off edge of sleeves to armhole edges.
Join side and sleeve seams. Sew cast on edge of collar to neck edge with the 14 straight rows of left side overlapping right side at centre front.

For illustration of **Norwegian Technique** sweater, see page 69

FAIRLY SIMPLE

MATERIALS

Pingouin 4 Pingouins

Shade No. 25 Marine (A)	10:	11:	11:	12: 50g balls
Shade No. 22 Perse (B)	2:	2:	2:	2: 50g balls
Shade No. 42 Ocre (C)	2:	2:	2:	2: 50g balls

Pair each 3¼mm and 3¾mm knitting needles.

MEASUREMENTS

To fit chest	97:	102:	107:	112:	cm
	38:	40:	42:	44:	in.
Actual measurements	107:	112:	117:	122:	cm
	42:	44:	46:	48:	in.
Length	58:	61.5:	64.5:	68:	cm
	23:	24½:	25½:	26¾:	in.
Sleeve length	48:	49:	50:	51:	cm
	18¾:	19¼:	19¾:	20:	in.

TENSION

24 sts and 44 rows = 10cm [4in.] over patt on 3¾mm needles.

ABBREVIATIONS

K = knit; P = purl; K1B [knit 1 below] = insert right-hand needle into next st one row below and knit it; A = 1st shade; B = 2nd shade; C = 3rd shade; sts = stitches; rep = repeat; patt = pattern; tog = together; sl 1 = slip 1; p.s.s.o. = pass slipped stitch over; dec = decrease; inc = increase; cm = centimetres; in. = inches.

BACK

With 3¼mm needles and A, cast on 127(133:139:145) sts.
1st row. K2, * P1, K1, rep from * to last st, K1.
2nd row. * K1, P1, rep from * to last st, K1.
Rep 1st and 2nd rows for 8cm [3¼in.] ending with 2nd row.

Change to 3¾mm needles and patt.
1st row [right side]. K.

2nd row. K1, * P1, K1B, rep from * to last 2 sts, P1, K1.
These 2 rows form patt.
Work until back measures 36(38:40:42)cm [14¼(15:15¾:16½)in.] from commencement, ending with 2nd patt row.

Shape raglan armholes.
1st row. K2 tog, K to last 2 sts, K2 tog.
Work 5 rows.
7th row. K4, sl 1, K2 tog, p.s.s.o., K to last 7 sts, K3 tog, K4.
Work 1 row.
Break off A and join in B.
Continue in stripes of 34 rows in B, 8 rows in A and 34 rows in C, *and at the same time* dec as 7th row at each end of the 6th row from previous dec, and then every 6th row until 93(99:105:111) sts remain, and then every 4th row until 61(67:73:79) sts remain.
Break off C and continue with A.
Dec as before at each end of next row, and then every 4th row until 41(43:45:47) sts remain.
Work 1 row.
Cast off.

FRONT

Follow instructions for back until
90(94:98:102) rows of raglan shaping
have been worked, and 55(55:57:59) sts
remain.

Shape neck.
Next row. K20 sts, cast off
13(15:17:19) sts, K to end.
Continue on last set of sts.
Continue to dec for raglan on 4th row

from previous dec, and following 4th row, and at the same time dec 1 st at neck edge on next 9 rows.
Next row. K3 tog, K4.
Next row. Patt 3, K2 tog.
Next row. [K2 tog] twice, pass 1st st over 2nd and fasten off.
With wrong side facing, rejoin yarn to remaining sts at neck edge and complete to match other side.

SLEEVES

With 3¼mm needles and A, cast on 61(65:69:73) sts.
Work 8cm [3¼in.] in rib as back.

Change to 3¾mm needles and patt.
Work 6 rows.
Inc 1 st at each end of next row, and then every 6th row until 77(81:85:89) sts and then every 8th row until 105(109:113:117) sts are on the needle.
Work until sleeve measures 48(49:50:51)cm [18¾(19¼:19¾:20)in.] from commencement, ending with 2nd patt row.

Shape top.
Work as for back, working stripes in same way.
Cast off 19 remaining sts.

MAKING UP

Press each piece lightly, following instructions on ball band.
Join front raglan seams, and right back seam, matching stripes.

Neck border.
With right side facing and 3¼mm needles and A, pick up and K 16 sts evenly from left sleeve top, 53(55:57:59) sts along front neck edge, 15 sts from right sleeve top and 41(43:45:47) sts along back neck edge. [125(129:133:137) sts.]
Work 4cm [1½in.] in rib as back welt, starting with 2nd row.
Cast off loosely in rib.
Join left back raglan and neck border seam.
Fold neck border in half on to wrong side and slip st loosely to picked up edge.
Join side and sleeve seams.
Press seams.

MATERIALS

Pingouin Confortable Sport
Shade No. 17 Gitane (A)   13 × 50g balls
Shade No. 40 Moravie (B)   6 × 50g balls

Pair each 3¾mm and 4½mm knitting needles.

MEASUREMENTS

To fit chest	102/107cm	40/42in.
Actual measurements	110cm	43in.
Length	63cm	25in.
Sleeve length	49cm	19¼in.

TENSION

19 sts and 20 rows = 10cm [4in.] over patt on 4½mm needles.

ABBREVIATIONS

K = knit; P = purl; st(s) = stitch(es); st. st. = stocking stitch; A = main; B = contrast; patt = pattern; beg = beginning; alt = alternate; dec = decrease; inc = increase; sl = slip; cm = centimetres; in. = inches.

BACK

With 3¾mm needles and A, cast on 94 sts.
Work 8cm [3¼in.] in K1, P1, rib.
Next row. P6, * P into front and back of next st, P7, rep from * to end. [105 sts.]

Change to 4½mm needles.
Continue in st. st. working in patt from chart.
1st row. K:[1A, 1B, 23A, 1B] 4 times, 1A.
2nd row. P:[1A, 2B, 21A, 2B] 4 times, 1A.
Continue in patt as set until 58 rows have been worked.
Start again at 7th row and inc 1 st at each end of this row to indicate commencement of armhole, keeping the extra st at each end in A.
Continue on these 107 sts until 110 rows have been worked in patt, thus completing 4th line of motifs. Work should measure approx 63cm [24¾in.] from commencement.
Continue with A.

Shape shoulders and back of neck.
Cast off 12 sts at beg of next 2 rows.
Next row. Cast off 12 sts, K14 sts including st on needle, cast off 31 sts, K to end.

Continue on last set of sts.
Next row. Cast off 12 sts, P to end.
Next row. Cast off 3 sts, K to end.
Cast off 11 remaining sts.
With wrong side facing, rejoin yarn to remaining sts at neck edge, cast off 3 sts, P to end.
Cast off 11 remaining sts.

FRONT

Work as back until 96 rows of patt have been worked.

Shape neck.
Next row. Patt 44, cast off 19, patt to end.
Continue on last set of sts.
Work 1 row.
** Cast off 3 sts at beg of next row and 2 sts at beg of following alt row.

Now dec 1 st at beg of every alt row until 35 sts remain. **

Work 1 more row to complete patt, and then continue with A.

Work 1 row.

Shape shoulder.
Cast off 12 sts at beg of next row, and following alt row.

Work 1 row.

Cast off 11 remaining sts.

With wrong side facing, rejoin yarn to remaining sts at neck edge, and follow instructions for other side from ** to **.

Work 2 more rows to complete patt. Continue with A, shaping shoulder as other side.

SLEEVES

Using 3¾mm needles and A, cast on 50 sts and work 8cm [3¼in.] in rib as back.

Next row. P5, * P into front and back of next st, P4, rep from * to end. [59 sts.]

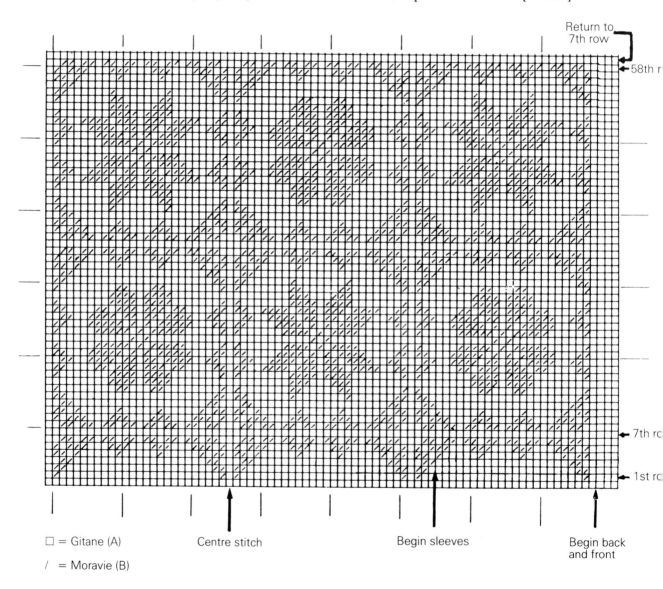

Return to 7th row

←58th r

←7th rc

←1st rc

□ = Gitane (A)

/ = Moravie (B)

Centre stitch

Begin sleeves

Begin back and front

Change to 4½mm needles.
Continue in st. st. and patt, starting with 3rd row which will read
K:[2B, 3A, 2B, 19A] twice, 2B, 3A, 2B.
Continue in patt as set.
Work 3 more rows.
Inc 1 st at each end of next row, and then every 4th row until 95 sts are on the needle.
Work 5 rows, ending with 28th patt row.
Now work 4 rows in A.
Cast off.

MAKING UP

Press each piece lightly following instructions on ball band.

Join right shoulder seam by backstitching.

Collar.
With 3¾mm needles and A, pick up and K 109 sts evenly round neck edge.
1st row. ★ K1, P1, rep from ★ to last st, K1.
2nd row. K2, ★ P1, K1, rep from ★ to last st, K1.
Rep 1st and 2nd rows for 12cm [4¾in.].
Cast off in rib.
Join left shoulder and collar seam.
Fold collar in half on to wrong side and sl st to picked up edge.
Join sleeves to armhole edges.
Join side and sleeve seams.
Press seams.

WITH YOKE

MATERIALS

Pingouin Confortable Sport

Shade No. 13 Cactus (A)	12:	13:	14:	15:	50g balls
Shade No. 41 Serbie (B)	2:	2:	2:	2:	50g balls
Shade No. 24 Grenat (C)	2:	2:	2:	2:	50g balls
Shade No. 40 Moravie (D)	1:	1:	1:	1:	50g ball
Shade No. 25 Pensée (E)	1:	1:	1:	1:	50g ball

Pair each 3¾mm and 4½mm knitting needles.
A zip fastener 20cm [8in.] long.

MEASUREMENTS

To fit chest	91:	97:	102:	107:	cm
	36:	38:	40:	42:	in.
Actual measurements	97:	104:	112:	117:	cm
	38:	41:	44:	46:	in.
Length	59.5:	62:	64.5:	67:	cm
	23½:	24½:	25½:	26½:	in.
Sleeve length to shoulder	50:	51:	52:	53:	cm
	19¾:	20:	20½:	20¾:	in.

TENSION

16 sts and 22 rows = 10cm [4in.] over st. st. on 4½mm needles. 18 sts and 20 rows = 10cm [4in.] over sleeve patt on 4½ mm needles.

ABBREVIATIONS

K = knit; P = purl; st(s) = stitch(es); A = main; B = 1st contrast; C = 2nd contrast; D = 3rd contrast; E = 4th contrast; st. st. = stocking stitch; beg = beginning; sl = slip; rep = repeat; alt = alternate; dec = decrease; inc = increase; patt = pattern; 0 = no sts in these sizes; cm = centimetres; in. = inches.

BACK

With 3¾mm needles and A, cast on 78(84:90:94) sts.
Work 7cm [2¾in.] in K1, P1, rib.

Change to 4½mm needles and st. st.
Continue until back measures 36(37:39:40)cm [14¼(14½:15½:15¾)in.] from commencement, ending with a P row.

Shape armholes.
Cast off 3(4:5:5) sts at beg of next 2 rows. [72(76:80:84) sts.]
Continue until armholes measure 24(25:26:27)cm [9½(9¾:10¼:10½)in.] from cast off sts, ending with a P row.

Shape shoulders and back of neck.
Cast off 7(7:8:8) sts at beg of next 2 rows.
Next row. Cast off 7(7:8:8) sts, K14(15:15:16) sts including st on needle, cast off 16(18:18:20) sts, K to end.

Continue on last set of sts.
Cast off 7(7:8:8) sts at beg of next row, and 8 sts at neck edge on following row.
Cast off 6(7:7:8) remaining sts.
With wrong side facing, rejoin yarn to remaining sts at neck edge, cast off 8 sts,

P to end.
Cast off 6(7:7:8) remaining sts.

FRONT

Follow instructions for back until front measures 39.5(41:44.5:46)cm [15½(16½:17½:18)in.] from commencement, ending with a P row.

Commence front opening.
1st row. K16(18:20:22) sts, turn leaving remaining sts on spare needle.
Continue on these sts until armhole measures same as back to shoulder, ending with a P row.

Shape shoulder.
Cast off 7(7:8:8) sts at beg of next row.
Work 1 row.
Cast off remaining 9(11:12:14) sts.
Return to sts left on spare needle, sl first 40 sts on to a st holder for yoke, rejoin yarn to remaining sts and K to end of row.
Complete as other side, working 1 row more to end at armhole edge before shaping shoulder.

YOKE

With 3¾mm needles and A, cast on 1 st, now with same needle and right side facing K across the first 20 sts at yoke edge as follows: [K2, P into front and back of next st] 6 times, K2, turn and cast on 1 st, leaving 20 remaining sts on st holder.
Continue on these 28 sts as follows:

1st row [wrong side]. K1, [P2, K2] 6 times, P2, K1.
2nd row. K3, [P2, K2] 6 times, K1.
Rep 1st and 2nd rows until work measures 16cm [6¼in.] from start of yoke, ending with a right side row.

Shape neck.
Cast off at beg of next and following alt rows 6(7:7:8) sts once, 4 sts once, 3 sts

WITH YOKE

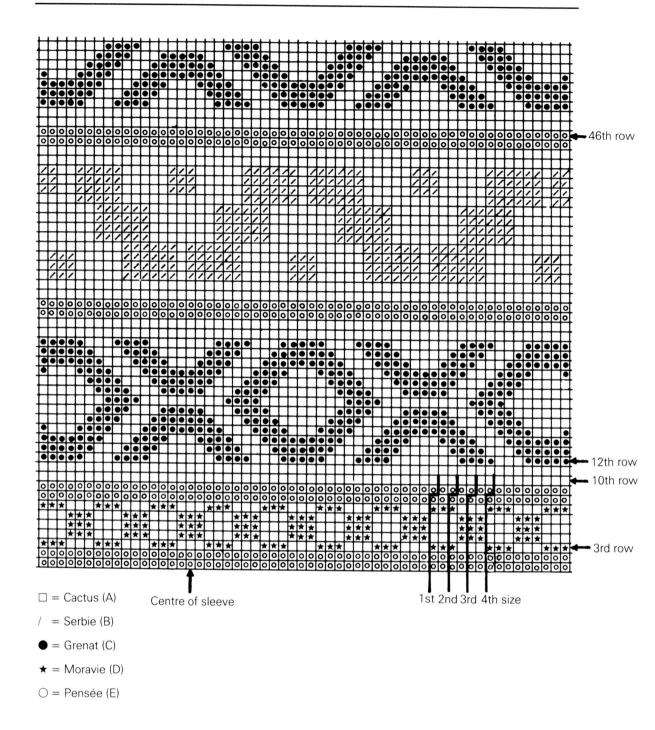

← 46th row

← 12th row
← 10th row

← 3rd row

□ = Cactus (A)

/ = Serbie (B)

● = Grenat (C)

★ = Moravie (D)

○ = Pensée (E)

Centre of sleeve

1st 2nd 3rd 4th size

Picture opposite: **With Yoke** sweater in Pingouin Confortable Sport

once and 2 sts twice, and then dec 1 st at beg of 2 following alt rows.

Work a few rows on the remaining 9(8:8:7) sts until work matches front to top of shoulder.

Cast off.

Work other side of yoke to match, reversing shapings.

SLEEVES

With 3¾mm needles and A, cast on 46(50:52:56) sts.

Work 5(6:7:8)cm [2(2¼:2¾:3¼)in.] in K1, P1, rib.

Next row. Rib 5(6:4:7), inc in next st, * rib 8(8:6:6), inc in next st, rep from * to last 4(7:5:6) sts, rib to end. [51(55:59:63) sts.]

Change to 4½mm needles.

Continue in st. st., working in patt from chart.

After working 2 rows in E as shown, arrange patt in the 3rd row as follows: K0(2:0:0)D, 3(3:1:3)A, * 3D, 3A, rep from * to last 6(2:4:6) sts, 3(2:3:3)D, 3(0:1:3)A.

Continue in patt as set.

Inc 1 st at each end of 9th patt row.

Work 2 rows. [53(57:61:65) sts.]

12th row. P0(0:1:3)C, 4(6:7:7)A, then 4C, 3A, 5C, 3A, 4C, 7A, 4C, 3A, 5C, 3A, 4C, 4(6:7:7)A, 0(0:1:3)C.

Now working the new sts in patt, inc 1 st at each end of next row and then every 4th row until 87(91:95:99) sts are on the needle, and *at the same time* when 46th row has been completed, work from 10th to 46th rows again.

Now work 3rd to 7th rows of chart with patt matching in the same way as at the beginning.

Work 3 rows in E.

Cast off.

MAKING UP

Press each piece lightly, following instructions on ball band.

Sew edges of yoke to edges of front opening.

Join shoulder seams.

Collar.

With 3¾mm needles and A, and with right side facing, pick up and K 84(88:88:92) sts along neck edge.

1st row. K1, * P2, K2, rep from * to last 3 sts, P2, K1.

2nd row. K3, * P2, K2, rep from * to last st, K1.

Rep 1st and 2nd rows for 12cm [4¾in.].

Cast off in rib.

Sew cast off edge of sleeves to side edges of armholes and cast off sts at underarms for a corresponding depth to side edges of sleeves.

Join side and sleeve seams.

Sew zip fastener at front opening with fastener extending partly along side edges of collar.

Fold collar in half on to wrong side and sl st cast off edge to picked up edge of neck, and then sew side edges to back of zip tapes.

Press seams.

MATERIALS

Pingouin Pingostar

Shade No. 608 Pekin (A)	8:	8:	9:	10:	10:	50g balls
Shade No. 531 Feu (B)	4:	4:	4:	5:	5:	50g balls

Pingouin Confortable Sport

Shade No. 43 Chaudron (C)	1:	1:	1:	1:	1:	50g ball

Pair each 3¼mm and 5mm knitting needles.

MEASUREMENTS

To fit chest	91:	97:	102:	107:	112:	cm
	36:	38:	40:	42:	44:	in.
Actual measurements	97:	102:	107:	112:	117:	cm
	38:	40:	42:	44:	46:	in.
Length	62:	64:	66:	68:	70:	cm
	24½:	25¼:	26:	26¾:	27½:	in.
Sleeve length	50:	50:	52:	52:	54:	cm
	19¾:	19¾:	20½:	20½:	21¼:	in.

TENSION

18 sts and 23 rows = 10cm [4in.] over patt on 5mm needles.

ABBREVIATIONS

K = knit; P = purl; A = main; B = 1st contrast; C = 2nd contrast; st(s) = stitch(es); st. st. = stocking stitch; beg = beginning; alt = alternate; inc = increase; cm = centimetres; in. = inches.

BACK

With 3¼mm needles and A, cast on 88(92:96:100:104) sts. Work 7cm [2¾in.] in K1, P1, rib.

Change to 5mm needles and st. st.
Work until back measures 38(39:40:41:42)cm [15(15½:15¾:16:16½)in.] from commencement, ending with a P row.
Break off A and join in C.

Shape armholes.
Cast off 3(4:4:5:5) sts at beg of next 2 rows. [82(84:88:90:94) sts.]
Work 6 more rows.
Break off C and join in B.
Work until back measures 62(64:66:68:70)cm [24½(25¼:26:26¾:27½) in.] from commencement, ending with a P row.

Shape shoulders and neck.
Cast off 9(9:9:10:10) sts at beg of next 2 rows.
Next row. Cast off 9(9:9:10:10) sts, K11(12:13:12:13) including st on needle, cast off 24(24:26:26:28) sts, K to end.
Next row. Cast off 9(9:9:10:10) sts, P to end.
Next row. Cast off 3 sts, K to end.
Cast off 8(9:10:9:10) remaining sts.
With wrong side facing, rejoin yarn to remaining sts at neck edge, cast off 3 sts, P to end.
Cast off 8(9:10:9:10) remaining sts.

FRONT

Follow instructions for back until front is 14 rows less than back to start of shoulder shaping.

Shape neck.
Next row. K36(37:38:39:40) sts, cast off
10(10:12:12:14) sts, K to end.
Continue in last set of sts.
Work 1 row.
★★ Cast off 3 sts at beg of next row, and
2 sts at beg of 2 following alt rows.
Now dec 1 st at beg of every alt row 3
times.
Work 2 rows, ending at armhole edge.

Shape shoulder.
Cast off 9(9:9:10:10) sts at beg of next
row, and following alt row.
Work 1 row.
Cast off 8(9:10:9:10) remaining sts.
With wrong side facing rejoin yarn to
remaining sts at neck edge and follow
instructions for other side from ★★ to
end.

SLEEVES

With 3¼mm needles and A, cast on
46(48:50:52:54) sts.
Work 7cm [2¾in.] in K1, P1, rib, inc
4(6:8:10:12) sts evenly spaced in last row.
[50(54:58:62:66) sts.]

Change to 5mm needles and st. st.
Work 4 rows.
Inc 1 st at each end of next row.

Work 3 rows.
Inc 1 st at each end of next row.
Work 5 rows.
Continue to inc in this way at each end
of next row, and then alternately on 4th
and 6th rows until 86(90:94:98:102) sts
are on the needle.
Work until sleeve measures
47(47:49:49:51)cm
[18½(18½:19¼:19¼:20)in.] from
commencement.
Break off A and work 8 rows in C.
Cast off.

MAKING UP

Press each piece lightly, following
instructions on ball band.
Join right shoulder seam.

Neck border.
With 3¼mm needles and right side
facing and using B, pick up and
K 99(99:103:103:107) sts evenly round
neck edge.
Work 2cm [¾in.] in K1, P1, rib.
Cast off in rib.
Join left shoulder and neck border seam.
Sew cast off edge of sleeves to armhole
edges.
Join side and sleeve seams.
Press seams.

Picture opposite: **For Beginners** sweater in
Pingouin Pingostar

MATERIALS

Pingouin Confortable Sport

Shade No. 13 Cactus (A)	9:	10:	10:	11:	11:	50g balls
Shade No. 41 Serbie (B)	6:	7:	7:	8:	8:	50g balls

Pair each 3¾mm and 5mm knitting needles.

MEASUREMENTS

To fit chest	91:	97:	102:	107:	112:	cm
	36:	38:	40:	42:	44:	in.
Actual measurements	102:	105:	110:	114:	119:	cm
	40:	41½:	43½:	45:	47:	in.
Length	61:	63:	65:	67:	69:	cm
	24:	24¾:	25½:	26¼:	27¼:	in.
Sleeve length	46:	47:	49:	50:	51:	cm
	18:	18½:	19¼:	19¾:	20:	in.

TENSION

18 sts and 19 rows = 10cm [4in.] over patt on 5mm needles.

ABBREVIATIONS

K = knit; P = purl; st(s) = stitch(es); st. st. = stocking stitch; rep = repeat; A = 1st shade; B = 2nd shade; inc = increase; 0 = no sts in this size; beg = beginning; patt = pattern; alt = alternate; dec = decrease; cm = centimetres; in. = inches.

BACK

★★ With 3¾mm needles and A, cast on 83(87:91:95:99) sts.
1st row. K2, ★ P1, K1, rep from ★ to last st, K1.
2nd row. ★ K1, P1, rep from ★ to last st, K1.
Rep 1st and 2nd rows for 8cm [3¼in.], ending with 2nd row.
Next row. K5(7:9:8:10) sts, inc in next st, ★ K11(11:11:12:12), inc in next st, rep from ★ to last 6(8:10:8:10) sts, K to end. [90(94:98:102:106) sts.]

Change to 5mm needles.
Next row. P. ★★
Continue in st. st., working from chart as follows:
[Strand yarn not in use loosely across wrong side of work over not more than 3 sts keeping fabric elastic.]

1st row. K0(2:4:6:8)A; then for 1st panel [1B, 1A, 3B, 3A] 3 times, 1B, 1A, 5B; then for 2nd panel [6A, 2B] 3 times, 9A; then [1B, 1A, 3B, 3A] 3 times, 1B, 1A, 0(2:4:5:5)B, 0(0:0:1:3)A.
Mark on chart the position where row ends for the size you are working; wrong side rows will begin at this position, working in reverse direction.

Continue in patt as set.
Work until back measures 61(63:65:67:69)cm [24(24¾:25½:26¼:27¼)in.] from commencement, ending with a wrong side row.

Shape shoulders.
Cast off 9(9:9:10:10) sts at beg of next 4 rows, and 9(10:11:10:11) sts at beg of 2 following rows.
Cast off 36(38:40:42:44) remaining sts.

FRONT

Follow instructions for back from
** to **.
Continue in st. st., working in patt from
chart as follows:
1st row [1st size]. K: 5A, * [2B, 6A]
twice, 2B, 9A, then work sts of 1st panel,
then [6A, 2B] 3 times, * 3A.
1st row [2nd size]. K: 1B, 6A, then from
* to * in 1st size, 5A.
1st row [3rd size]. K: 3B, 6A, then from
* to * in 1st size, 7A.
1st row [4th size]. K: 5B, 6A, then from
* to * in 1st size, 9A.
1st row [5th size]. K: 1B, 1A, 5B, 6A,
then from * to * in 1st size, 9A, 1B, 1A.

Continue in patt as set.
Work until front is 14 rows less than
back to start of shoulders.

Shape neck.
Next row. Patt 36(37:38:39:40) sts, cast
off 18(20:22:24:26) sts, patt to end.
Continue on last set of sts.
Work 1 row.
Cast off 3 sts at beg of next row, and
2 sts at beg of 2 following alt rows, now
dec 1 st at beg of next 2 alt rows.
Work 4 rows on 27(28:29:30:31)
remaining sts, ending at arm edge.

Shape shoulder.
Cast off 9(9:9:10:10) sts at beg of next
row, and following alt row.
Work 1 row.
Cast off 9(10:11:10:11) remaining sts.
With wrong side facing, rejoin yarn to
remaining sts at neck edge and complete
to match other side.

RIGHT SLEEVE

** With 3¾mm needles and A, cast on
47(49:51:53:55) sts.
Work 7cm [2¾in.] in rib as back, ending
with 2nd row.
Next row. K2(3:4:5:6) sts, inc in next st,
* K6, inc in next st, rep from * to last
2(3:4:5:6) sts, K to end.
[54(56:58:60:62) sts.]

Change to 5mm needles.
Next row. P. **
Continue working in patt from chart.
1st row. K: 0(0:0:0:1)B, 3(4:5:6:6)A, [2B,
6A] twice, 2B, 9A, [1B, 1A, 3B, 3A] 3
times; then **for 2nd size** 1B; **for 3rd size**
1B, 1A; **for 4th size** 1B, 1A, 1B; **for 5th
size** 1B, 1A, 2B.
Mark chart at beg and end of rows for
the size you are working.

Continue in patt as set.
Work 3 more rows.
Now working the new sts in patt, inc 1 st
at each end of next row, and then every
4th row until 84(86:84:84:86) sts are on
the needle.
Now inc 1 st at each end of 1(1:3:4:4)
following 6th rows. [86(88:90:92:94) sts.]
Work until sleeve measures
46(47:49:50:51)cm
[18(18½:19¼:19¾:20)in.] from
commencement.
Cast off.

LEFT SLEEVE

Follow instructions for right sleeve from
** to **.
Continue working in patt from chart.
1st row [1st size]. * K: [3B, 3A, 1B, 1A] 3
times, 5B, [6A, 2B] 3 times, * 1A.
1st row [2nd size]. K: 1A, then from
* to * in 1st size, 2A.
1st row [3rd size]. K: 1B, 1A, then from
* to * in 1st size, 3A.
1st row [4th size]. K: 1A, 1B, 1A, then
from * to * in 1st size, 4A.
1st row [5th size]. K: 2A, 1B, 1A, then
from * to * in 1st size, 5A.
Continue in patt as set.
Complete as right sleeve.

FOR MOUNTAINEERS

MAKING UP

Press each piece lightly, following instructions on ball band.
Join right shoulder seam.

Neck border.

With 3¾mm needles and right side facing, pick up and K 52(54:56:58:60) sts along front neck edge, and 36(38:40:42:44) sts along back neck edge.

[88(92:96:100:104) sts.]
Work 7 rows in K1, P1, rib.
Cast off in rib. Join left shoulder and neck border seam.
Place a marker 24(24.5:25:26:26.5)cm [9½(9¾:10:10¼:10½)in.] on each side of shoulder seams to mark depth of armholes.
Join cast off edge of sleeves to armhole edges.
Join side and sleeve seams.
Press seams.

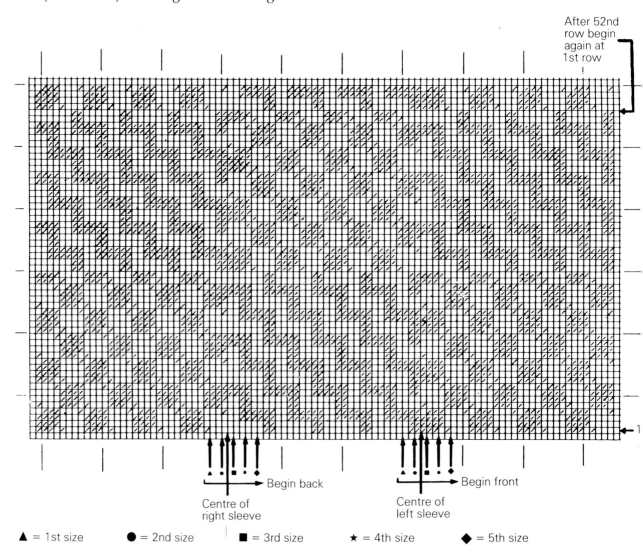

After 52nd row begin again at 1st row

← 1

→ Begin back

Centre of right sleeve

→ Begin front

Centre of left sleeve

▲ = 1st size   ● = 2nd size   ■ = 3rd size   ★ = 4th size   ◆ = 5th size

□ = Cactus (A)

/ = Serbie (B)

Picture opposite: **For Mountaineers** sweater in Pingouin Confortable Sport

COLOUR HARMONY

MATERIALS

Pingouin Sport Laine

1st shade No. 512 Amiral (A)	9:	10:	10:	11:	12:	50g balls
2nd shade No. 511 Petrolé (B)	5:	6:	6:	7:	7:	50g balls
3rd shade No. 507 Moravie (C)	2:	2:	2:	2:	3:	50g balls

Pair each 3¼mm and 4mm knitting needles.

MEASUREMENTS

To fit chest	91:	97:	102:	107:	112:	cm
	36:	38:	40:	42:	44:	in.
Actual measurements	102:	107:	112:	117:	122:	cm
	40:	42:	44:	46:	48:	in.
Length	62:	64:	65:	66:	67:	cm
	24½:	25¼:	25½:	26:	26½:	in.
Sleeve length to shoulder	50:	51:	51:	52:	52:	cm
	19¾:	20:	20:	20½:	20½:	in.

TENSION

19 sts and 22 rows = 10cm [4in.] over
st. st. on 4mm needles.

ABBREVIATIONS

K = knit; P = purl; st(s) = stitch(es);
st. st. = stocking stitch; A = 1st shade; B
= 2nd shade; C = 3rd shade; rep =
repeat; inc = increase; patt = pattern; 0
= no sts in this size; dec = decrease; beg
= beginning; alt = alternate; cm =
centimetres; in. = inches.

BACK

With 3¼mm needles and A, cast on
91(95:99:103:107) sts.
1st row. K2, * P1, K1, rep from * to
last st, K1.
2nd row. * K1, P1, rep from * to last st,
K1.
Rep 1st and 2nd rows for 6(7:7:8:8)cm
[2¼(2¾:2¾:3¼:3¼)in.], ending with 1st
row.
Next row. P9(8:7:9:8), inc in next st,
* P11(12:13:13:14), inc in next st, rep

from * to last 9(8:7:9:8) sts, P to end.
[98(102:106:110:114) sts.]

Change to 4mm needles.
Continue in st. st. and colour patt.
1st row. K: 0(1:3:0:0)B, 3(4:4:1:3)A, * 4B,
4A, rep from * to last 7(1:3:5:7) sts,
4(1:3:4:4)B, 3(0:0:1:3)A.
Continue in patt as set, working from
chart.
On 35th row the patt will read
K: 0(2:4:0:2)B, * 2C, 4B, rep from * to last
2(4:6:2:4) sts, 2C, 0(2:4:0:2)B.
On 50th row which is worked in A, dec
1 st in centre of row.
[97(101:105:109:113) sts.]
51st row [1st size only]. K: * [1B, 5A, 5B,
5A] 6 times, 1B*.
51st row [2nd size only]. K: 2A, then
work from * to * as 1st size, 2A.
51st row [3rd size only]. K: 4A, then
work from * to * as 1st size, 4A.
51st row [4th size only]. K: 1B, 5A, then
work from * to * as 1st size, 5A, 1B.
51st row [5th size only]. K: 3B, 5A, then
work from * to * as 1st size, 5A, 3B.
Continue in patt until back measures
37(38:38:39:39)cm

[14½(15:15:15½:15½)in.] from commencement, ending with a P row.

Shape armholes.
Cast off 5(5:6:6:7) sts at beg of next 2 rows.
Continue on remaining
87(91:93:97:99) sts until the panel marked D has been completed, inc 1 st in centre of last row.
Continue on 88(92:94:98:100) sts until the 87th row of patt has been worked.
88th row. P: 4(0:1:3:4)B, ★2C, 4B, rep from ★ to last 6(2:3:5:6) sts, 2C, 4(0:1:3:4)B.
Continue in patt until last row of chart has been worked, and then start again with 1st row which will now be a P row.
Arrange blocks on 1st row so as to have 4A at centre in same way as at start of patt.
Continue until back measures 62(64:65:66:67)cm [24½(25¼:25½:26:26½)in.] from commencement, ending with a P row.

Shape shoulders and neck.
Cast off 9(9:9:10:10) sts at beg of next 2 rows.
Next row. Cast off 9(9:9:10:10) sts, patt 13(14:15:14:14) sts including st on needle, cast off 26(28:28:30:32) sts, patt to end.
Continue on last set of sts.
Cast off 9(9:9:10:10) sts at beg of next row, and 5 sts at neck edge on following row.
Cast off remaining 8(9:10:9:9) sts.
With wrong side facing, rejoin yarn to remaining sts at neck edge, cast off 5 sts, work to end.
Cast off remaining 8(9:10:9:9) sts.

FRONT

Work as back until front is 12 rows less than back to start of shoulders, ending with a P row.

Shape neck.
Next row. Patt 39(40:41:42:42) sts, cast

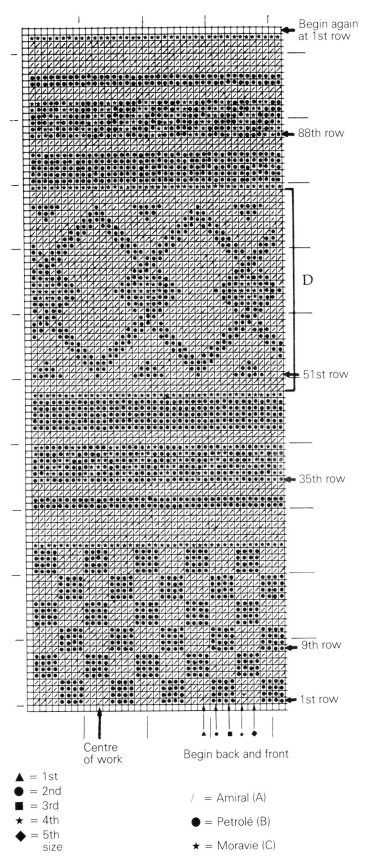

Begin again at 1st row

88th row

D

51st row

35th row

9th row

1st row

Centre of work

Begin back and front

▲ = 1st
● = 2nd
■ = 3rd
★ = 4th
◆ = 5th
size

/ = Amiral (A)
● = Petrolé (B)
★ = Moravie (C)

off 10(12:12:14:16) sts, patt to end.
Continue on last set of sts.
Work 1 row.
★★ Cast off at beg of next and following
alt rows at neck edge, 3 sts twice and
2 sts 3 times and then dec 1 st at beg of
following alt row, ending at armhole
edge.

Shape shoulder.
Cast off 9(9:9:10:10) sts at beg of next
row, and following alt row.
Work 1 row.
Cast off remaining 8(9:10:9:9) sts.
With wrong side facing, rejoin yarn to
remaining sts at neck edge and follow
instructions for other side from ★★ to
end.

SLEEVES

With 3¼mm needles and A, cast on
49(51:55:55:57) sts and work 6(7:7:8:8)cm
[2¼(2¾:2¾:3¼:3¼)in.] in rib as back,
ending with 1st row.
Next row. P6(4:6:6:4), inc in next st,
★ P8(6:6:6:5), inc in next st, rep from ★ to
last 6(4:6:6:4) sts, P to end.
[54(58:62:62:66) sts.]

Change to 4mm needles.
Continue in st. st. and colour patt,
starting with 9th row as follows:
K0(0:1:1:3)A, 1(3:4:4:4)B, ★ 4A, 4B, rep
from ★ to last 5(7:1:1:3) sts, 4(4:1:1:3)A,
1(3:0:0:0)B.
Continue in patt as set.
Work 5 more rows.

Inc 1 st at each end of next row, and
then the following 6th row, and then 1 st
at each end of every 4th row 18 times,
working extra sts into patt. *At the same
time* dec 1 st in centre of 50th row of
chart, then on following row arrange
motifs so as to have a diamond in the
centre. Inc 1 st in centre of last row of
panel marked **D.**
When all incs have been completed
continue in patt on 94(98:102:102:106) sts
until sleeve measures 50(51:51:52:52)cm
[19¾(20:20:20½:20½)in.] from
commencement.
Cast off.

MAKING UP

Press each piece lightly, following
instructions on ball band.
Join right shoulder seam.

Neck border.
With 3¼mm needles and A, and with
right side facing, pick up and
K 61(63:63:65:67) sts along front neck
edge, and 40(42:42:44:46) sts along back
neck edge. [101(105:105:109:113) sts.]
Work 4 rows in rib as welt, starting with
2nd row.
Cast off.
Join left shoulder and neck border seam.
Join cast off edge of sleeves to side edges
of armholes, and cast off sts at
underarms for a corresponding depth to
side edges of sleeves.
Join side and sleeve seams.
Press seams.

Picture opposite: **Colour Harmony** sweater in
Pingouin Sports Laine

ABACUS

MATERIALS

Scheepjeswol Superwash Zermat
Main shade 4812 White   13:   14: 50g balls
Contrast shade 4822 Grey   3:   3: 50g balls

Pair each 3¼mm and 4½mm knitting needles.

MEASUREMENTS

To fit chest	99/104:	107/112:	cm
	39/41:	42/44:	in.
Actual measurements	113:	121:	cm
	44½:	47½:	in.
Length	65:	66:	cm
	25½:	26:	in.
Sleeve length	52:	53.5:	cm
	20½:	21:	in.

TENSION

21 sts and 26 rows = 10cm [4in.] over st. st. on 4½mm needles.

ABBREVIATIONS

K = knit; P = purl; st(s) = stitch(es); st. st. = stocking stitch; M = main; C = contrast; M1 = inc 1 st by picking up strand between last st worked and next st and work into back of it; rep = repeat; patt = pattern; dec = decrease; inc = increase; alt = alternate; cm = centimetres; in. = inches.

BACK

** With 3¼mm needles and M, cast on 108(114) sts.
Work 6cm [2¼in.] in K1, P1, rib.
Next row. Rib 5(5), M1, * rib 9(8), M1, rep from * to last 4(5) sts, rib to end. [120(128) sts.]

Change to 4½mm needles.
Join in C and continue in patt.
[Strand yarn not in use loosely across wrong side of work, keeping fabric elastic.]

1st row. K: * 2C, 2M, rep from * to end.
2nd and following alt rows. P: working in same colours as previous row.
Rep 1st and 2nd rows 3 times more.
9th row. K: *2M, 2C, rep from * to last 4 sts, 4M.
11th row. With M, K.
13th row. As 1st row.
15th row. As 9th row.
16th row. As 2nd row.
Rep 15th and 16th rows 3 times more.
23rd and 24th rows. As 1st and 2nd rows.
25th row. As 11th row.
27th row. K: *2M, 2C, rep from * to last 8(16) sts, 8(16)M.
29th row. K: *2C, 2M, rep from * to last 12(20) sts, 2C, 10(18)M.
30th row. As 2nd row.
Rep 29th and 30th rows 3 times more.
37th row. K: *2M, 2C, rep from * to last 12(20) sts, 12(20)M.
39th row. As 11th row.
41st row. K: *2C, 2M, rep from * to last 28(36) sts, 2C, 26(34)M.
43rd row. K: *2M, 2C, rep from * to last 28(36) sts, 28(36)M.
44th row. As 2nd row.
Rep 43rd and 44th row 3 times more.
51st row. K: *2C, 2M, rep from * to last 32(40) sts, 2C, 30(38)M.

53rd row. As 11th row.
55th row. K: *2M, 2C, rep from * to last 44(52) sts, 44(52)M.
57th row. K: *2C, 2M, rep from * to last 48(56) sts, 2C, 46(54)M.
58th row. As 2nd row.
Rep 57th and 58th rows 3 times more.
65th row. K: [2M, 2C] 18 times, 48(56)M.
67th row. As 11th row.
69th row. K: [2C, 2M] 14 times, 2C, 62(70)M.
71st row. K: [2M, 2C] 14 times, 64(72)M.
72nd row. As 2nd row.
Rep 71st and 72nd rows 3 times more.
79th row. K: [2C, 2M] 13 times, 2C, 66(74)M.
81st row. With M: K.

Shape armholes.
82nd row. With M: cast off 6 sts, P to last 6 sts, cast off these sts. Break yarn.
Turn and rejoin yarn to remaining sts.
83rd row. K: [2C, 2M] 8 times, 2C, 74(82)M.
85th row. K: [2M, 2C] 8 times, 76(84)M.
86th row. As 2nd row.
Rep 85th and 86th rows 3 times more.
93rd row. K: [2C, 2M] 7 times, 2C, 78(86)M.
95th row. As 11th row.
97th row. K: [2M, 2C] 4 times, 92(100)M.
99th row. K: [2C, 2M] 3 times, 2C, 94(102)M.
100th row. As 2nd row.
Rep 99th and 100th rows 3 times more.
107th row. K: [2M, 2C] 3 times, 96(104)M.
108th row. P: 96(104)M, [2C, 2M] 3 times. **
Continue in st. st. with M.
Work 34(36) rows.
Cast off.

FRONT

Follow instructions for back from ** to ** but reading patt rows in reverse.
Continue in st. st. with M.
Work 12(14) rows.

Shape neck.
Next row. K46(50) sts, turn leaving remaining sts on spare needle.
Continue on these sts.
Dec 1 st at neck edge on next 8 rows, and then the 5 following alt rows.
Work 3 rows.
Cast off 33(37) remaining sts.
With right side facing, rejoin yarn to remaining sts at neck edge, cast off centre 16 sts, K to end.
Complete to match other side.

SLEEVES

With 3¼mm needles and M, cast on 54(56) sts.
Work 5cm [2in.] in K1, P1, rib.
Next row. Rib 4(5), M1, * rib 5, M1, rep from * to last 5(6) sts, rib to end. [64(66) sts.]

Change to 4½mm needles and st. st.
Work 4 rows.
Inc 1 st at each end of next row, and then every 6th row until 102(106) sts are on the needle.
Work until sleeve measures 52(53)cm [20½(21)in.] from commencement, ending with a P row. Cast off loosely.

MAKING UP

Press each piece lightly following instructions on ball band.
Place a marker on the 33rd(37th) st from each arm edge at cast off edge of back to mark back of neck.
Join right shoulder seam.

Neck border.
With 3¼mm needles and M, and with right side facing, pick up and K 25 sts evenly down left side of front neck edge, 16 sts from the cast off sts, 25 sts up right side of neck, and 46 sts evenly between the markers at back of neck.
Work 2.5cm [1in.] in K1, P1, rib.
Cast off in rib.

ABACUS

Join left shoulder and neck border seam.   Join side and sleeve seams.
Join cast off sleeve edges to armhole edges.   Press seams.

MATERIALS

Pingouin Pingofrance
Shade No. 131 Feu   12:   13:   14:   15:   16:   50g balls

Pair each 3mm and 4mm knitting needles. A cable needle.

MEASUREMENTS

To fit chest	86:	91:	97:	102:	107:	cm
	34:	36:	38:	40:	42:	in.
Actual measurements	97:	102:	107:	112:	117:	cm
	38:	40:	42:	44:	46:	in.
Length	59:	62:	65:	67:	69:	cm
	23¼:	24½:	25½:	26½:	27:	in.
Sleeve length	45:	46:	48:	49:	50:	cm
	17¾:	18:	18¾:	19¼:	19¾:	in.

TENSION

23 sts and 30 rows = 10cm [4in.] over double moss st on 4mm needles.

ABBREVIATIONS

K = knit; P = purl; st(s) = stitch(es); patt = pattern; M1P = inc 1 st by picking up strand between last st worked and next st and P into back of it; M1K = increase 1 st by picking up strand between last st worked and next st, and K it, but not through the back; sl = slip; p.s.s.o. = pass slipped st over; tog = together; rep = repeat; inc = increase; beg = beginning; alt = alternate; cm = centimetres; in. = inches.

THE MAIN PATTERN
[worked over a multiple of 17 sts plus 14 sts]

1st row [right side]. * P2, [K2, P2] 3 times, K1, P1, K1, * [P2, K2] 3 times, P2.
2nd row. * K2, [P2, K2] 3 times, P1, K1, P1* [K2, P2] 3 times, K2.
3rd row. * P2, [K2, P2] 3 times, [K1, M1P] twice, K1, * [P2, K2] 3 times, P2.
4th row. * K2, [P2, K2] 3 times, [P1, K1] twice, P1, *[K2, P2] 3 times, K2.

5th row. * P2, [K2, P2] 3 times, K1, M1P, K1, P1, K1, M1P, K1, * [P2, K2] 3 times, P2.
6th row. * K2, [P2, K2] 3 times, [P1, K1] 3 times, P1, *[K2, P2] 3 times, K2.
7th row. * P2, [K2, P2] 3 times, K1, M1P, [K1, P1] twice, K1, M1P, K1, * [P2, K2] 3 times, P2.
8th row. * K2, [P2, K2] 3 times, [P1, K1] 4 times, P1, *[K2, P2] 3 times, K2.
9th row. * P2, [K2, P2] 3 times, K1, M1P, [K1, P1] 3 times, K1, M1P, K1, * [P2, K2] 3 times, P2.
10th row. * K2, M1K, then keeping yarn at back [right side of work] sl next 10 sts purlwise, then pass the K loop over last 10 sts and off the needle, [which will have the effect of drawing the work together], K2, [P1, K1] 5 times, P1, * K2, M1K, sl next 10 sts purlwise, pass the K loop over last 10 sts and off the needle, K2.
11th row. * P2, [K2, P2] 3 times, sl 1, K1, p.s.s.o., [P1, K1] 3 times, P1, K2 tog, * [P2, K2] 3 times, P2.
12th row. As 8th.
13th row. * P2, [K2, P2] 3 times, sl 1, K1, p.s.s.o., [P1, K1] twice, P1, K2 tog, * [P2, K2] 3 times, P2.
14th row. As 6th.
15th row. * P2, [K2, P2] 3 times, sl 1, K1,

p.s.s.o., P1, K1, P1, K2 tog, * [P2, K2] 3 times, P2.

16th row. As 4th.

17th row. * P2, [K2, P2] 3 times, sl 1, K1, p.s.s.o., P1, K2 tog, * [P2, K2] 3 times, P2.

18th row. As 2nd.

19th row. * P2, [K2, P2] 3 times, sl next st on to cable needle and hold at front, now pass needle in front of next st, lift up following st and K it leaving it on needle, then P the 1st st and sl both off the needle, then K1 from cable needle * [P2, K2] 3 times, P2.

20th row. As 2nd.

The 3rd to 20th rows form the patt.

Note.

Additional sts are made on 3rd, 5th, 7th and 9th rows, and these are eliminated on 11th, 13th, 15th and 17th rows. Throughout work, if counting total of sts, each patt panel must be counted as 17 sts.

During shapings, if casting off over the section of patt where diamond is formed and there are extra sts, work these tog during casting off to obtain correct number of sts.

BACK

With 3mm needles cast on 117(123:127:133:137) sts.

1st row. K2, * P1, K1, rep from * to last st, K1.

2nd row. * K1, P1, rep from * to last st, K1.

Rep 1st and 2nd rows for 8cm [3¼in.] ending with 1st row.

Next row. Rib 2(7:9:6:8), inc in next st, * rib 6(5:5:5:5), inc in next st, rep from * to last 2(7:9:6:8) sts, rib to end. [134(142:146:154:158) sts.]

Change to 4mm needles and patt.

1st row. K1, [P1, K1] 4(6:7:9:10) times, now rep from * to * of 1st row of main patt 6 times, then work last 14 sts of main patt, then [K1, P1] 4(6:7:9:10) times, K1.

2nd row. P1, [K1, P1] 4(6:7:9:10) times, now rep from * to * of 2nd row of main patt 6 times, then work last 14 sts, then [P1, K1] 4(6:7:9:10) times, P1.

3rd row. P1, [K1, P1] 4(6:7:9:10) times, now rep from * to * of 3rd row of main patt 6 times, then work last 14 sts, then [P1, K1] 4(6:7:9:10) times, P1.

4th row. K1, [P1, K1] 4(6:7:9:10) times, now rep from * to* of 4th row of main patt 6 times, then work last 14 sts, then [K1, P1] 4(6:7:9:10) times, K1.

These 6 rows form double moss st patt for remainder of back.

Continue over the centre 116 sts in main patt, with remainder in double moss st. Work until back measures 35(37:39:40:41)cm [13¾(14½:15¼:15¾:16¼)in.] from commencement, ending with a wrong side row.

Shape armholes.

Cast off 8(10:11:13:14) sts at beg of next 2 rows.

Work until armholes measure 24(25:26:27:28)cm [9½(10:10¼:10¾:11)in.] from cast off sts, ending with a wrong side row.

Shape shoulders and neck.

Cast off 11(12:12:12:13) sts at beg of next 2 rows.

Next row. Cast off 11(12:12:12:13) sts, patt 22(21:22:23:22) sts including st on needle, [counting sts of diamond always as 3 sts], cast off 30(32:32:34:34) sts, patt to end.

Continue on last set of sts.

Cast off 11(12:12:12:13) sts at beg of next row, and 10 sts at neck edge on following row.

Cast off 12(11:12:13:12) remaining sts. With wrong side facing, rejoin yarn to remaining sts at neck edge, cast off

10 sts, patt to end.
Cast off 12(11:12:13:12) remaining sts.

FRONT

Follow instructions for back until armholes are 16 rows less than back to start of shoulders ending with a wrong side row.

Shape neck.
Next row. Patt 51(52:53:54:55) sts, cast off 16(18:18:20:20) sts, patt to end.

Continue on last set of sts.
Work 1 row.
★★ Cast off 4 sts at beg of next row and following alt row, and 2 sts at beg of 3 following alt rows; now dec 1 st at beg of next 3 alt rows at neck edge, ending at armhole edge.
Shape shoulder as back.
With wrong side facing, rejoin yarn to remaining sts at neck edge and follow instructions for other side from ★★ to end.

SLEEVES

With 3mm needles cast on 59(63:63:67:67) sts.
Work 8cm [3¼in.] in rib as back, ending with 1st row.
Next row. Rib 2(4:4:6:6) sts, inc in next st, ★ rib 2, inc in next st, rep from ★ to last 2(4:4:6:6) sts, rib to end.
[78(82:82:86:86) sts.]

Change to 4mm needles and patt.
1st row [1st size only]. [K2, P2] 3 times, K1, P1, K1, rep from ★ to ★ of 1st row of patt 3 times, [P2, K2] 3 times, thus there is an incomplete patt panel at each side for this size.
1st row (2nd and 3rd sizes only]. Rep from ★ to ★ of 1st row of patt 4 times, then work last 14 sts of patt.
1st row [4th and 5th sizes only]. P1, K1, then rep from ★ to ★ of 1st row of patt 4 times, then work last 14 sts of patt and then K1, P1.

Continue in patt as set.
Work 3 rows.
Inc 1 st at each end of next row, and then the 3(3:2:3:2) following 6th rows, and then 1 st at each end of every 4th row until 126(132:136:140:144) sts are on the needle.
Work until sleeve measures 48(50:52:54:56)cm [19(19¾:20½:21¼:22)in.] from commencement, ending with a wrong side row.
Cast off.

Note.
For the 1st size the first 2 sts increased will complete the main patt.
For this and other sizes remainder of increased sts can either be worked in main patt or double moss st.

MAKING UP

Press each piece lightly, following instructions on ball band.
Join right shoulder seam.

Neck border.
Using 3mm needles, and with right side facing, pick up and K 109(113:113:117:117) sts round neck edge.
Work 10 rows in rib as welt, starting with 2nd row.
Cast off in rib.
Join left shoulder and neck border seam.
Fold neck border in half on to wrong side and slip st to picked up edge.
Sew cast off edge of sleeves to side edges of armholes, and the cast off sts at underarms to corresponding depth at sleeve edges.
Join side and sleeve seams.
Press seams.

MATERIALS

Wendy Family Choice Chunky

Main shade 524 Cream Aran	16:	17:	18:	50g balls
1st contrast shade 513 Mediterranean	2:	2:	2:	50g balls
Wendy Family Choice D.K.				
2nd contrast shade 238 Verd Antique	1:	1:	1:	50g ball

Pair each 5mm and 6mm knitting needles. A 5mm circular knitting needle. A 5mm crochet hook.

MEASUREMENTS

To fit chest	97:	102:	107:	cm
	38:	40:	42:	in.
Actual measurements	107:	112:	117:	cm
	42:	44:	46:	in.
Length	68:	68:	69:	cm
	26¾:	26¾:	27¼:	in.

TENSION

15 sts and 20 rows = 10cm [4in.] over st. st. on 6mm needles.

ABBREVIATIONS

K = knit; P = purl; st(s) = stitch(es); st. st. = stocking stitch; M = main; A = 1st contrast; B = 2nd contrast; rep = repeat; inc = increase; dec = decrease; alt = alternate; tog = together; cm = centimetres; in. = inches.

SWEATER IS WORKED IN ONE PIECE

Commence at left cuff edge.
With 5mm needles and M, cast on 34(34:36) sts.
1st row. * P2, K2, rep from * to last 2 sts, P2.
2nd row. * K2, P2, rep from * to last 2 sts, K2.
Rep 1st and 2nd rows for 6cm [2¼in.], ending with 2nd row.

Change to 6mm needles.
Next row [1st and 2nd sizes only]. K into front and back of first st, * K2, K into front and back of next st, rep from * to end.
Next row [3rd size only]. K1, K into front and back of next st, * K2, K into front and back of next st, rep from * to last st, K1. [46(46:48) sts.]
Continue in st. st., starting with a P row. Work 3 rows.
Inc 1 st at each end of next row, and then every 6th row until 72(72:74) sts, and then every 4th row until 78(80:82) sts are on the needle.
Work 1 row.
Next row. Cast on 51(51:51) sts, K to end.
Now with a separate strand of yarn cast on 51(51:51) sts and K these sts on to end of last row. [180(182:184) sts.]
Work 11(13:17) rows.
Now continue in st. st., but working in stripes of 4 rows in A, and 16 rows in M. Work 22 rows.

Shape neck.
Next row. K90(91:92) sts, cast off 2 sts, K to end.
Continue on last set of sts, leaving remainder on a spare needle.

Dec 1 st at neck edge on next 4 rows, and then the 3 following alt rows.
Work 19 rows.
Inc 1 st at neck edge on next row, and then the 3 following alt rows, and then 1 st on every row 3 times, ending at neck edge.
Turn and cast on 2 sts. Break off yarn.
With wrong side facing, rejoin yarn to remaining sts at neck edge.
Work 39 rows.
Next row. K to end, and then K across sts on spare needle.
Work 21 rows.
The 5th A stripe should now be completed.

Continue with M.
Work 12(14:18) rows.
Next row. Cast off 51(51:51) sts, K to last 51(51:51) sts.
Cast off these sts. Break yarn.
Turn and rejoin yarn to remaining sts.
Work 1 row.
Dec 1 st at each end of next row, and then every 4th row until 70(70:72) sts remain, and then every 6th row until 46(46:48) sts remain.
Work 2 rows.
Next row [1st and 2nd sizes only].
* P2 tog, P2, rep from * to last 2 sts, P2 tog.
Next row [3rd size only]. P1, * P2 tog, P2, rep from * to last 3 sts, P2 tog, P1. [34(34:36) sts.]
Change to 5mm needles and work 6cm [2¼in.] in rib as first cuff.
Cast off in rib.

FRONT WELT

With 5mm needles and M and right side facing, pick up and K 74(78:82) sts evenly along lower edge (approx 2 sts for each 3 rows).
1st row. [K2, P2] 1(1:2) times, * K2 tog, K1, P2, K2, P2, rep from * to last 7(11:11) sts, K2 tog, K1 [P2, K2] 1(2:2) times. [66(70:74) sts.]
2nd row. * P2, K2, rep from * to last 2 sts, P2.
3rd row. * K2, P2, rep from * to last 2 sts, K2.
Rep 2nd and 3rd rows until welt measures 8cm [3¼in.] from picked up edge. Cast off in rib. Work back welt the same.

COLLAR

With 5mm circular needle, and M and right side facing, pick up and K 84 sts evenly along neck edge.
Work 21cm [8¼in.] in rounds of K2, P2, rib.
Cast off in rib.
Using 5mm crochet hook and 2 strands of B, work diagonal stripes in chain st on front and back as shown in photograph.
Join side and sleeve seams.
Press seams.

For illustration of **Knitted Sideways** sweater, see page 101

MATERIALS

Pingouin Corrida 4
Shade 502   13:   14:   50g balls

Pair each 3¼mm and 4½mm knitting needles. A cable needle.

MEASUREMENTS

To fit chest	94/99:	99/104:	cm
	37/39:	39/41:	in.
Actual measurements	107:	112:	cm
	42:	44:	in.
Length	67:	68:	cm
	26½:	27:	in.
Sleeve length	51:	51:	cm
	20:	20:	in.

TENSION

19 sts and 29 rows = 10cm [4in.] over patt on 4½mm needles.

ABBREVIATIONS

K = knit; P = purl; st(s) = stitch(es); rep = repeat; patt = pattern; C10F [cable 10 front] = slip next 5 sts on to cable needle and hold at front, K5, then K5 from cable needle; tog = together; beg = beginning; alt = alternate; dec = decrease; inc = increase; cm = centimetres; in. = inches.

BACK

With 3¼mm needles cast on 102(106) sts.
1st row. * P2, K2, rep from * to last 2 sts, P2.
2nd row. * K2, P2, rep from * to last 2 sts, K2.
Rep 1st and 2nd rows for 6cm [2½in.] ending with 2nd row.

Change to 4½mm needles and patt.
1st row. * K1, P1, rep from * to end.
2nd row. * P1, K1, rep from * to end.
Rep 1st and 2nd rows 1(2) times more.

Larger size only.
Next row. As 1st row.
Following row. P2, * P1, K1, rep from * to last 2 sts, P2.

Continue for both sizes.
1st row. K1(3), * P1, K1, rep from * to last 1(3) sts, K1(3).
2nd row. P2(4), * P1, K1, rep from * to last 2(4) sts, P2(4).
3rd row. K3(5), * P1, K1, rep from * to last 3(5) sts, K3(5).
4th row. P2(4), K2, * P1, K1, rep from * to last 4(6) sts, K2, P2(4).
5th row. K5(7), * P1, K1, rep from * to last 5(7) sts, K5(7).
Continue with the centre panel in moss st in this way, working 1 st less at each side in every row.
6th row. P2(4), K2, P2, moss st to last 6(8) sts, P2, K2, P2(4).
7th row. K7(9), moss st to last 7(9) sts, K7(9).
8th row. P2(4), K2, P4, moss st to last 8(10) sts, P4, K2, P2(4).
9th row. K9(11), moss st to last 9(11) sts, K9(11).
10th row. P2(4), K2, P4, K2, moss st to last 10(12) sts, K2, P4, K2, P2(4).
11th row. K11(13), moss st to last 11(13) sts, K11(13).

12th row. P2(4), K2, P4, K2, P2, moss st to last 12(14) sts, P2, K2, P4, K2, P2(4).
13th row. K13(15), moss st to last 13(15) sts, K13(15).
14th row. P2(4), K2, P4, K2, P4, moss st to last 14(16) sts, P4, K2, P4, K2, P2(4).
15th row. K15(17), moss st to last 15(17) sts, K15(17).
16th row. P2(4), K2, P4, K2, P6, moss st to last 16(18) sts, P6, K2, P4, K2, P2(4).
17th row. K17(19) sts, moss st to last 17(19) sts, K17(19).
18th row. P2(4), K2, P4, K2, P8, moss st to last 18(20) sts, P8, K2, P4, K2, P2(4).
19th row. K19(21) sts, moss st to last 19(20) sts, K19(21).
20th row. P2(4), K2, P4, K2, P10, moss st to last 20(22) sts, P10, K2, P4, K2, P2(4).
21st row. K21(23), moss st to last 21(23) sts, K21(23).
22nd row. P2(4), K2, P4, K2, P10, K2, moss st to last 22(24) sts, K2, P10, K2, P4, K2, P2(4).
23rd row. K23(25), moss st to last 23(25) sts, K23(25).
24th row. P2(4), K2, P4, K2, P10, K2, P2, moss st to last 24(26) sts, P2, K2, P10, K2, P4, K2, P2(4).
Work 8 more rows, working 2 sts less in moss st in the centre, and working the extra sts at sides into rib patt as before.
33rd row. K10(12), C10F, K13, moss st 36, K13, C10F, K10(12).
Work 17 more rows, working 2 sts less in moss st in the centre, and the extra sts at sides in rib patt and working C10F as before on following 12th row.
51st row. K.
52nd row. P2(4), K2, P4, K2, P10, [K2, P4] 4 times, K2, P10, [K2, P4] 4 times, K2, P10, K2, P4, K2, P2(4).
Work 4 more rows in patt as set.
57th row. K10(12), C10F, K26, C10F, K26, C10F, K10(12).
Work 3 more rows in patt.
61st row. K.
62nd row. P2(4), K2, P4, K2, P10, [K2, P4] 4 times, K2, P10, K2, [P4, K2] 4 times, P10, K2, P4, K2, P2(4).
63rd row. K.

64th row. P2(4), K2, P4, K2, P10, [K2, P4] 4 times, P1, K1, P10, K1, P1, [P4, K2] 4 times, P10, K2, P4, K2, P2(4).
65th row. K.
66th row. P2(4), K2, P4, K2, P10, [K2, P4] 3 times, K2, P3, K1, P1, K1, P10, K1, P1, K1, P3, [K2, P4] 3 times, K2, P10, K2, P4, K2, P2(4).
67th row. K.
68th row. P2(4), K2, P4, K2, P10, [K2, P4] 3 times, K2, P2, [P1, K1] twice, P10, [K1, P1] twice, P2, K2, [P4, K2] 3 times, P10, K2, P4, K2, P2(4).
69th row. As 57th row.
Continue to work 1 st less in rib patt at each side and the extra sts in broken rib on every alt row in this way, and keeping 3 cable panels as before.
Work 41 more rows.
There are now 25 sts at each side of centre cable in broken rib.
111th row. K20(22), K2 tog, K58, K2 tog, K20(22). [100(104) sts.]
112th row. P2(4), K2, P4, K2, P10, [K1, P1] 12 times, K1, P10, [K1, P1] 12 times, K1, P10, K2, P4, K2, P2(4).
Work 23 more rows in patt as set.
136th row. P2(4), K2, P5, K1, P10, [K1, P1] 12 times, K1, P10, [K1, P1] 12 times, K1, P10, K1, P5, K2, P2(4).
137th row. K.
138th row. P2(4), K2, P3, K1, P1, K1, P10, [K1, P1] 12 times, K1, P10, [K1, P1] 12 times, K1, P10, K1, P1, K1, P3, K2, P2(4).
Continue in this way, working 1 st more in broken rib at each side on every alt row.
Work 17 more rows.
Work 19 rows in patt as now set.
Cast off, marking the 31st(33rd) st from each arm edge.
Centre 38 sts are for back of neck.

FRONT

Follow instructions for back until front is 26 rows less than back to shoulders.

Shape neck.
Next row. K44(46) sts, cast off 12 sts, K to end.
Continue on last set of sts.
Work 1 row.
** Cast off at beg of next and following alt rows at neck edge, 4 sts once, 3 sts once and 2 sts once, and then dec 1 st at beg of 4 following alt rows.
Work 11 rows. Cast off 31(33) remaining sts.
With wrong side facing, rejoin yarn to remaining sts at neck edge and follow instructions for other side from ** to end.

SLEEVES

With 3¼mm needles cast on 40 sts.
1st row. P1, K2, * P2, K2, rep from * to last st, P1.
2nd row. K1, P2, * K2, P2, rep from * to last st, K1.
Rep 1st and 2nd rows for 6cm [2½in.] ending with 1st row.
Next row. Inc in first st, * rib 2, inc in next st, rep from * to end. [54 sts.]

Change to 4½mm needles.
1st row. [K1, P1] 11 times, K10, [P1, K1] 11 times.
2nd row. [K1, P1] 11 times, P10, [P1, K1] 11 times.
Continue with 1 cable in the centre, and the remainder in moss st, and working C10F on the 7th, and every following 12th row, and *at the same time* inc 1 st at each end of the 5th row, and then every 4th row until 66 sts, and then every 6th row until 98 sts are on the needle.
Work until sleeve measures 51cm [20in.] from commencement, ending with a wrong side row.
Cast off.

MAKING UP

Press each piece lightly, following instructions on ball band.
Join right shoulder seam.

Neck border.
With 3¼mm needles and right side facing, pick up and K 104 sts evenly round neck edge.
1st row. K1, P2, * K2, P2, rep from * to last st, K1.
2nd row. P1, K2, * P2, K2, rep from * to last st, P1.
Rep last 2 rows for 3cm [1¼in.].
Cast off in rib.
Join left shoulder and neck border seams.
Place a marker 26cm [10¼in.] on each side of shoulder seams to mark depth of armholes.
Join cast off edge of sleeves to armhole edges.
Join side and sleeve seams.
Press seams.

MATERIALS

Poppleton Plaza D.K. shade 859 Alhambra   12:   13: 50g balls
Pair each 3¼mm and 4mm knitting needles.

MEASUREMENTS

To fit chest	97/102:	104/109:	cm
	38/40:	41/43:	in.
Actual measurements	109:	117:	cm
	43:	46:	in.
Length	65:	68:	cm
	25½:	26¾:	in.
Sleeve length	50:	51.5:	cm
	19¾:	20¼:	in.

TENSION

20 sts and 40 rows = 10cm [4in.] over patt on 4mm needles.

ABBREVIATIONS

K = knit; K1B [K1 below] = insert right hand needle into next st 1 row below and K it; P = purl; st(s) = stitch(es); rep = repeat; M1 = inc 1 st by picking up strand between last st worked and next st, and work into back of it; patt = pattern; inc = increase; cm = centimetres; in. = inches.

BACK

With 3¼mm needles cast on 101(109) sts.
1st row. K2, * P1, K1, rep from * to last st, K1.
2nd row. * K1, P1, rep from * to last st, K1.
Rep 1st and 2nd rows for 7cm [2¾in.], ending with 1st row.
Next row. Rib 7(5), M1, * rib 8(9), M1, rep from * to last 6(5) sts, rib to end. [113(121) sts.]

Change to 4mm needles and patt.
1st row [right side]. K1(5), * P1, K9, [P1, K1B] 5 times, rep from * to last 12(16) sts, P1, K9, P1, K1(5).
2nd row. P1(5), K1B, * P9, [K1B, P1] 5 times, K1B, rep from * to last 11(15) sts, P9, K1B, P1(5).
3rd row [smaller size only]. K1, * P11, [K1B, P1] 4 times, K1B, rep from * to last 12 sts, P11, K1.
3rd row [larger size only]. K1, [P1, K1B] twice, * P11, [K1B, P1] 4 times, K1B, rep from * to last 16 sts, P11, [P1, K1B] twice, K1.
4th row [smaller size only]. K1, K1B, * K9, [K1B, P1] 5 times, K1B, rep from * to last 11 sts, K9, K1B, P1.
4th row [larger size only]. K1, [K1B, P1] twice, K1B, * K9, [K1B, P1] 5 times, K1B, rep from * to last 15 sts, K9, [K1B, P1] twice, K1B, K1.
Rep 1st to 4th rows 3 times more, and then 1st and 2nd rows once.
19th row. K1(5), * [P1, K1B] 5 times, P1, K9, rep from * to last 12(16) sts, [P1, K1B] 5 times, P1, K1(5).
20th row. P1(5), * [K1B, P1] 5 times, K1B, P9, rep from * to last 12(16) sts, [K1B, P1] 5 times, K1B, P1(5).
21st row. K1(5), P1, * [K1B, P1] 4 times, K1B, P11, rep from * to last 11(15) sts, [K1B, P1] 5 times, K1(5).
22nd row. K1(5), * [K1B, P1] 5 times, K1B, K9, rep from * to last 12(16) sts, [K1B, P1] 5 times, K1B, K1(5).

Rep 19th to 22nd rows 3 times more, and then 19th and 20th rows once.
These 36 rows form the patt.
Work until back measures 61(64)cm [24(25¼)in.] from commencement, ending with a wrong side row.
Change to 3¼mm needles and work 4cm [1½in.] in rib as welt.
Cast off in rib.

FRONT

Work as back.

SLEEVES

With 3¼mm needles cast on 49(49) sts and work 7cm [2¾in.] in rib as back, ending with 1st row.
Next row. Rib 3, M1, * rib 4, M1, rep from * to last 2 sts, rib 2. [61 sts.]

Change to 4mm needles.
Work in patt as 2nd size back.

Work 6 rows.
Now working the new sts in patt, inc 1 st at each end of next row, and then every 6th row until 111(115) sts are on the needle.
Work until sleeve measures 50(51.5)cm [19¾(20¼)in.] from commencement, ending with a wrong side row.
Cast off in patt.

MAKING UP

Press each piece lightly, following instructions on ball band.
Join shoulder seams, leaving neck open as required.
Place a marker 28(29)cm [11(11½)in.] on each side of shoulder seams to mark depth of armholes.
Join cast off edge of sleeves to armhole edges.
Join side and sleeve seams.
Press seams.

MATERIALS

Scheepjes Voluma shade 5374 Light Blue   4:   5:   5:   6: 50g balls
Pair each 3mm and 3¾mm knitting needles.

MEASUREMENTS

To fit chest	92/94:	97/99:	102/104:	107/109:	cm
	36/37:	38/39:	40/41:	42/43:	in.
Length	61:	63:	64:	66:	cm
	24:	25:	25¼:	26:	in.

TENSION

24 sts and 32 rows = 10cm [4in.] over patt on 3¾mm needles.

ABBREVIATIONS

K = knit; P = purl; st(s) = stitch(es); rep = repeat; patt = pattern; sl 1P = slip 1 purlwise; dec = decrease; cm = centimetres; in. = inches; tog = together.

FRONT

** With 3mm needles cast on 111(119:127:135) sts.
1st row. K2, * P1, K1, rep from * to last st, K1.
2nd row. * K1, P1, rep from * to last st, K1.
Rep 1st and 2nd rows for 5cm [2in.], ending with 2nd row.

Change to 3¾mm needles and patt.
1st row. * K3, sl 1P with yarn at back, rep from * to last 3 sts, K3.
2nd row. P.
These 2 rows form patt.
Work until front measures 38(39.5:39.5:41)cm [15(15½:15½:16)in.] from commencement, ending with a wrong side row.

Shape armholes.
Next row. Cast off 6 sts, patt to last 6 sts, cast off these sts.
Break yarn. **
Turn and rejoin yarn to remaining sts.
Work 5 rows.

Divide for neck.
Next row. Patt 49(53:57:61) sts, turn leaving remaining sts on spare needle.

Continue on these sts.
Work 2 rows.
Dec 1 st at neck edge on next row, and then every 3rd row until 30(32:36:38) sts remain.
Work 10(6:8:4) rows without shaping.
Cast off.
Leave centre st on a safety pin, rejoin yarn to remaining sts and patt to end.
Complete to match other side.

BACK

Follow instructions for front from ** to **.
Work until back measures same as front to shoulders, ending with a wrong side row.
Cast off, marking centre 39(43:43:47) sts for back of neck.

EASY RIB PATTERN

MAKING UP

Do not press. Join right shoulder seam.

Neck border.
With 3mm needles and right side facing, pick up and K 51(53:55:55) sts evenly down left side of front neck edge, (approx 6 sts for 8 rows), K st from safety pin, pick up and K 50(52:54:54) sts up right side of neck, and 39(43:43:47) sts along back neck edge.
1st row. * K1, P1, rep from * to within 1 st of st picked up at point of V, P3 tog, rib to end.
2nd row. Rib to within 1 st of picked up st, K3 tog, rib to end.

Work 8 more rows in rib, at the same time dec in this way on every row.
Cast off in rib, dec as before.
Join left shoulder seam.

ARMHOLE BORDERS

With 3mm needles and right side facing, pick up and K 111(115:117:121) sts along straight edge of armhole, omitting cast off sts.
Work 10 rows in rib as welt, starting with 2nd row.
Cast off in rib.
Join side edges of borders to cast off sts.
Join side seams.

CASUAL WEAR

MATERIALS

Scheepjeswol Linnen shade 261 White	14:	15:	16:	50g balls

Pair each 3¼mm and 4mm knitting needles.

MEASUREMENTS

To fit chest	91/97:	102/107:	112/117:	cm
	36/38:	40/42:	44/46:	in.
Actual measurements	108:	116:	124:	cm
	42½:	45½:	49:	in.
Length	64:	67:	70:	cm
	25:	26¼:	27½:	in.
Sleeve length	51:	53.5:	53.5:	cm
	20:	21:	21:	in.

TENSION

19 sts and 25 rows = 10cm [4in.] over st. st. on 4mm needles.

ABBREVIATIONS

K = knit; P = purl; st(s) = stitch(es); st. st. = stocking stitch; inc = increase; rep = repeat; patt = pattern; dec = decrease; alt = alternate; tog = together; 0 = no sts in these sizes; cm = centimetres; in. = inches.

Note.
Garment is worked in double yarn throughout.

FRONT

With 3¼mm needles and using 2 strands of yarn together cast on 94(100:106) sts. Work 6cm [2¼in.] in K1, P1, rib.
Next row. Rib 4(4:3), inc in next st, ★ rib 11(9:8), inc in next st, rep from ★ to last 5(5:3) sts, rib to end. [102(110:118) sts.]

Change to 4mm needles and commence patt.

2nd size only.
1st row. P81, K29.
2nd row. P29, K81.
Rep 1st and 2nd rows 3 times more.
3rd size only.
1st row. K.
2nd row. P.
Rep 1st and 2nd rows 3 times more.
9th row. P85, K33.
10th row. P33, K85.
Rep 9th and 10th rows 3 times more.

Continue for all sizes.
1st row. K.
2nd row. P.
Rep 1st and 2nd rows 3 times more.
9th row. P70(74:78), K32(36:40).

10th row. P32(36:40), K to end.
Rep 9th and 10th rows 3 times more.
17th row. K.
18th row. P.
Rep 17th and 18th rows 3 times more.
25th row. P63(67:71), K15, P7, K17(21:25).
26th row. P17(21:25), K7, P15, K63(67:71).
Rep 25th and 26th rows 3 times.
33rd row. K71(75:79), P7, K24(28:32).
34th row. P24(28:32), K7, P71(75:79).
Rep 33rd and 34th rows 3 times more.
41st row. P56(60:64), K8, P7, K31(35:39).
42nd row. P31(35:39), K7, P8, K56(60:64).
Rep 41st and 42nd rows 3 times more.
49th row. K71(75:79), P7, K7, P7, K10(14:18).
50th row. P10(14:18), K7, P7, K7, P71(75:79).
Rep 49th and 50th rows 3 times more.
57th row. P49(53:57), K29, P7, K17(21:25).
58th row. P17(21:25), K7, P29, K49(53:57).
Rep 57th and 58th rows 3 times more.
65th row. K.
66th row. P.
Rep 65th and 66th rows 3 times more.
73rd row. P42(46:50), K60(64:68).
74th row. P60(64:68), K42(46:50).
Rep 73rd and 74th rows 3 times more.
81st row. K57(61:65), P7, K28, P7, K3(7:11).
82nd row. P3(7:11), K7, P28, K7, P57(61:65).
Rep 81st and 82nd rows 3 times more.
89th row. P35(39:43), K15, P7, K28, P7, K10(14:18).
90th row. P10(14:18), K7, P28, K7, P15, K35(39:43).
Rep 89th and 90th rows 3 times more.
97th row. K43(47:51), P7, K28, P7, K17(21:25).
98th row. P17(21:25), K7, P28, K7, P43(47:51).
Rep 97th and 98th rows 3 times more.
105th row. P28(32:36), K22, P7, K7, P7,

K14, P7, K7, P3(7:7), K0(0:4).
106th row. P0(0:4), K3(7:7), P7, K7, P14, K7, P7, K7, P22, K28(32:36).
Rep 105th and 106th rows 3 times more.
113th row. K57(61:65), P7, K28, P7, K3(7:11).
114th row. P3(7:11), K7, P28, K7, P57(61:65).
Rep 113th and 114th rows 3 times more.
121st row. P21(25:29), K to end.
122nd row. P to last 21(25:29) sts, K to end.
Rep 121st and 122nd rows once more.

Shape neck.
Next row. P21(25:29), K23, cast off 14, K to end.

Continue on last set of sts in st. st.
Dec 1 st at neck edge on next 6 rows, and then the 5 following alt rows.
Work 3 rows.
Cast off 33(37:41) remaining sts.
With wrong side facing, rejoin yarn to remaining sts at neck edge.
1st row. P2 tog, P to last 21(25:29) sts, K to end.
2nd row. P21(25:29), K to last 2 sts, K2 tog.
3rd row. As 1st row.
4th row. K to last 2 sts, K2 tog.
5th row. P2 tog, P to end.
Work 6 more rows in st. st., at the same time dec 1 st at neck edge on next row, and following alt rows.
Next row. P14(18:22), K to last 2 sts, K2 tog.
Following row. P to last 14(18:22) sts, K to end.
Rep last 2 rows twice more.
Work 2 rows without shaping.
Cast off remaining sts.

BACK

Follow instructions for front, reading patt rows in reverse, and omitting neck shaping. Cast off, marking the 33rd(37th:41st) st from each arm edge for back of neck.

SLEEVES

With 3¼mm needles and using 2 strands of yarn together cast on 52(52:52) sts.
Work 6cm [2¼in.] in K1, P1, rib.
Next row. Rib 3, inc in next st, * rib 4, inc in next st, rep from * to last 3 sts, rib 3. [62 sts.]

Change to 4mm needles and continue in st. st.
Work 4 rows.
Inc 1 st at each end of next row, and then every 5th row until 104(108:108) sts are on the needle.
Work until sleeve measures 51(53.5:53.5)cm [20(21:21)in.] from commencement, ending with a wrong side row.
Cast off loosely knitwise.

MAKING UP

Press each piece lightly, following instructions on ball band.
Join right shoulder seam.

Neck border.
With 3¼mm needles and right side facing, pick up and K 20 sts down left side of front neck edge, 14 sts from the cast off sts, 20 sts up right side of neck, and 36 sts between the markers at back of neck. [90 sts.]
Work 2.5cm [1in.] in K1, P1, rib.
Cast off loosely in rib.
Join left shoulder and neck border seam.
Place a marker 27(28.5:28.5)cm [10¾(11¼:11¼)in.] on each side of shoulder seams to mark depth of armholes.
Join cast off edge of sleeves to armhole edges.
Join side and sleeve seams.
Press seams.

MATERIALS

Schaffhauser Sunday shade 35 Marmot   14:   15: 50g balls

Pair each 3mm and 3½mm knitting needles. A 3mm circular knitting needle. A cable needle. 5 buttons.

MEASUREMENTS

To fit chest	97/102:	104/109:	cm
	38/40:	41/43:	in.
Actual measurements	108:	114:	cm
	42½:	45:	in.
Length	68:	69:	cm
	26¾:	27¼:	in.
Sleeve length	51:	51:	cm
	20:	20:	in.

TENSION

24 sts and 30 rows = 10cm [4in.] over st. st. on 3¾mm needles.

ABBREVIATIONS

K = knit; P = purl; st(s) = stitch(es); st. st. = stocking stitch; rep = repeat; M1 = inc 1 st by picking up strand between last st worked and next st, and work into back of it; sl = slip; C16B [cable 16 back] = sl next 8 sts on to cable needle and hold at back, K8, then K8 from cable needle; patt = pattern; dec = decrease; beg = beginning; alt = alternate; inc = increase; cm = centimetres; in. = inches.

LEFT FRONT

With 3mm needles cast on 58(62) sts.
1st row [wrong side]. K1, * P2, K2, rep from * ending K3, instead of K2.
Rep 1st row for 8cm [3¼in.], ending with a right side row.
Next row. Rib 1(3), M1, * rib 4, M1, rep from * to last 1(3) sts, rib 1(3). [73(77) sts.]

Change to 3¾mm needles and patt.

1st row. K1, P5(6), * K16, P6(7), rep from * to last st, K1.
2nd row. K1, * K6(7), P16, rep from * to

last 6(7) sts, K6(7).
3rd to 10th rows. Rep 1st and 2nd rows 4 times.
11th row. K1, P5(6), * sl next 8 sts on to cable needle and hold at back, K8, then K8 from cable needle [*referred to as C16B*], P6(7), rep from * to last st, K1.
12th row. As 2nd row.
13th to 22nd rows. Rep 1st and 2nd rows 5 times.
These 22 rows form patt.
Work until the 22nd row of the 4th patt has been completed.

Shape front slope.
Next row. Patt to last 3 sts, dec 1 st, K1.
Continue to dec in this way at end of every 4th row twice more.
Work 1 row.
The 10th row of the 5th patt should now be completed.
Next row. K1, P5(6), * C16B, P6(7), rep from * once more, sl next 8 sts on to cable needle and hold at back, K6, K2 tog, then K2 tog, K6, from cable needle, work to end. [14 sts in last cable.]
The last cable is now kept in st. st. throughout.
Work 1 row.
Continue to dec for front slope within the edge st on next and following 4th rows until 20 decs in all have been made, *and at the same time* reduce centre cable to 14 sts on the 11th row of the 6th patt, and then keep these 14 sts in st. st.; then reduce the remaining cable to 14 sts on the 11th row of the 7th patt, keeping them in st. st.
When front slope shaping is completed, work until front measures 65(67)cm [25½(26)in.] from commencement, ending at arm edge.

Shape shoulder.
Cast off 10(10) sts at beg of next row, and 9(10) sts at beg of 3 following alt rows.
Work 1 row.
Cast off 10(11) remaining sts.

RIGHT FRONT

With 3mm needles cast on 58(62) sts.
1st row [wrong side]. K3, P2, * K2, P2, rep from * to last st, K1.
Rep 1st row for 8cm [3¼in.], ending with a right side row.
Work inc row as left front.

Change to 3¾mm needles and patt.
1st row. K1, * P6(7), K16, rep from * to last 6(7) sts, P5(6), K1.
Continue in patt as set until the 22nd row of the 4th patt has been completed.

Shape front slope.
Next row. K1, dec 1 st, patt to end.
Complete to match left front, reversing shapings, and working 1 row more to end at arm edge before shaping shoulder.

BACK

With 3mm needles cast on 124(132) sts.
1st row [wrong side]. K1, P2, * K2, P2, rep from * to last st, K1.
2nd row. P1, K2, * P2, K2, rep from * to last st, P1.
Rep 1st and 2nd rows for 8cm [3¼in.], ending with 1st row.
Next row [smaller size only]. Rib 4, M1, * rib 6, M1, rib 5, M1, rep from * to last 10 sts, rib 6, M1, rib 4.
Next row [larger size only]. Rib 3, M1, * rib 6, M1, rep from * to last 3 sts, rib 3. [146(154) sts.]

Change to 3¾mm needles and patt.
1st row [right side]. K1, P5(6), K14, * P6(7), K14, rep from * to last 6(7) sts, P5(6), K1.
2nd row. K6(7), * P14, K6(7), rep from * to end.
These 2 rows form patt.
Work until back measures same as fronts to shoulders, ending with a wrong side row.
Shape shoulders and back of neck.
Cast off 10(10) sts at beg of next 2 rows and 9(10) sts at beg of next 2 rows.

Next row. Cast off 9(10) sts, patt 22(24) sts including st on needle, turn leaving remaining sts on spare needle.

Continue on these sts.
Dec 1 st at neck edge on next 3 rows, and at the same time cast off 9(10) sts at beg of following alt row at shoulder edge.
Cast off 10(11) remaining sts.
With right side facing rejoin yarn to remaining sts at neck edge, cast off centre 46 sts, patt to end.
Dec 1 st at neck edge on next 3 rows, and at the same time cast off 9(10) sts at beg of next row, and following alt row.
Work 1 row.
Cast off 10(11) remaining sts.

SLEEVES

With 3mm needles cast on 62(62) sts.
1st row. * P2, K2, rep from * to last 2 sts, P2.
2nd row. * K2, P2, rep from * to last 2 sts, K2.
Rep 1st and 2nd rows for 8cm [3¼in.], ending with 1st row.
Next row. Rib 4, M1, * rib 2, M1, rep from * to last 4 sts, rib 4. [90 sts.]
Change to 3¾mm needles and work in patt of 18 rows in reverse st. st. [P1 row, K1 row alternately] and 4 rows in st. st. [K1 row, P1 row alternately], and at the same time, continue as follows:

Smaller size only.
Work 14 rows.
Inc 1 st at each end of next row, and then every 6th row until 130 sts are on the needle.
Work 3 rows, ending with 22nd patt row.
Cast off.

Larger size only.
Work 18 rows.
Inc 1 st at each end of next row, and then alternately on following 4th and 6th rows until 136 sts are on the needle.

Work 5 rows, ending with 22nd patt row.
Cast off.

MAKING UP

Press each piece lightly, following instructions on ball band.
Join shoulder seams.

Border.
With the 3mm circular needle and starting in the cast on row of right front, pick up and K 22 sts evenly along edge of ribbing, 78 sts along centre front edge to first shaping for front slope, and 79(83) sts along shaped edge to shoulder (approx 7 sts for 8 rows); 54 sts along back neck edge, 79(83) sts along shaped edge of left front, 78 sts to top of ribbing and 22 sts evenly along edge of ribbing. [412(420) sts.]
1st row. K1, P2, * K2, P2, rep from * to last st, K1.
2nd row. K3, * P2, K2, rep from * to last st, K1.
These 2 rows form rib.
Work until border measures 2.5cm [1in.] from picked up edge, ending with 2nd row.
Next row. Rib 5, make buttonhole as follows: Sl next 2 sts purlwise on to right-hand needle, pass first of these 2 sts over the 2nd and off the needle; sl 3rd st from left-hand needle on to right-hand needle, and then sl the 2nd st over the 3rd st; rep in this way on 4th and 5th sts, and then sl 5th st back on to left-hand needle [thus casting off 4 sts without knitting them], turn and cast on 4 sts, * rib 18, make buttonhole, rep from * 3 times more, rib to end.
Continue in rib until border measures 5cm [2in.] from picked up edge.
Cast off in rib.
Place a marker 27(28)cm [10½(11)in.] on each side of shoulder seams to mark depth of armholes.
Join cast off edge of sleeves to armhole edges.
Join side and sleeve seams.
Press seams.
Sew on buttons.

MATERIALS

Wendy Dolce shade 472 Maple Syrup	8:	8:	9:	9:	50g balls
Wendy Pampas shade 581 Silk Grass	6:	6:	7:	7:	50g balls

Pair each 4mm and 5mm knitting needles.

MEASUREMENTS

To fit chest	97:	102:	107:	112:	cm
	38:	40:	42:	44:	in.
Actual measurements	104:	109:	114:	119:	cm
	41:	43:	45:	47:	in.
Length	63.5:	66:	67.5:	69:	cm
	25:	26:	26½:	27:	in.
Sleeve length	51.5:	53:	53:	53:	cm
	20¼:	20¾:	20¾:	20¾:	in.

TENSION

18 sts and 25 rows = 10cm [4in.] over patt on 5mm needles.

ABBREVIATIONS

K = knit; P = purl; st(s) = stitch(es); rep = repeat; M1 = inc 1 st by picking up strand between last st worked and next st, and K into back of it; inc = increase; patt = pattern; dec = decrease; cm = centimetres; in. = inches; tog = together; tbl = through back of loops; sl = slip; p.s.s.o. = pass slipped st over.

Garment is worked using 1 strand of each yarn together throughout.

FRONT

** With 4mm needles cast on 85(89:93:97) sts.
1st row. K2, * P1, K1, rep from * to last st, K1.
2nd row. * K1, P1, rep from * to last st, K1.
Rep 1st and 2nd rows for 7cm [2¾in.], ending with 1st row.

Change to 5mm needles.

Next row. K6(8:2:4), M1, * K8, M1, rep from * to last 7(9:3:5) sts, rib to end. [95(99:105:109) sts.]

Continue in patt.
1st row. K2, * P1, K1, rep from * to last st, K1.
2nd row. * K1, P1, rep from * to last st, K1.
3rd row. As 1st row.
4th row. K.
These 4 rows form patt.**
Work until front measures 42(44.5:46:47)cm [16½(17½:18:18½)in.] from commencement, ending with a wrong side row.

Divide for neck.
Next row. Patt 47(49:52:54) sts, turn leaving remaining sts on spare needle.

Continue on these sts.
Work 1 row.
Dec 1 st at neck edge on next row.
Work 3 rows.
Dec 1 st at neck edge on next row.
Work 1 row.
Continue to dec at neck edge in this way on next row, and following 4th and 2nd rows alternately until 29(31:33:35) sts remain.

Work 1 row. Cast off.
Leave centre st on a st holder, rejoin yarn to remaining sts, work to end.
Complete to match other side.

BACK

Follow instructions for front from
** to **.
Work until back is 8 rows less than front to shoulders.

Shape back of neck.
Next row. Patt 36(38:40:42) sts, cast off 23(23:25:25) centre sts, patt to end.
Continue on last set of sts.
Dec 1 st at neck edge on next 7 rows.
Cast off remaining sts.
With wrong side facing, rejoin yarn to remaining sts at neck edge and complete to match other side.

SLEEVES

With 4mm needles cast on 41(41:43:43) sts and work 7cm [2¾in.] in rib as front, ending with 1st row.

Change to 5mm needles.
Next row. K1(1:2:2), M1, ★ K3, M1, K2, M1, rep from ★ to last 5(5:6:6) sts, K3, M1, K2(2:3:3). [57(57:59:59) sts.]

Continue in patt.
Work 4 rows.
Inc 1 st at each end of next row, and then every 4th row until 65(65:69:69) sts, and then every 6th row until 91(91:95:95) sts are on the needle.
Work until sleeve measures 51.5(53:53:53)cm [20¼(20¾:20¾:20¾)in.] from commencement, ending with a wrong side row.
Cast off loosely.

MAKING UP

Press each piece lightly, following instructions on ball band.
Join right shoulder seam.

Neck border.
With 4mm needles and right side facing, pick up and K 47(47:49:49) sts down left side of front neck edge [approx 5 sts for 6 rows], K st on st holder, 47(47:49:49) sts up right side of neck, and 42(42:44:44) sts along back neck edge.
1st row. K1, ★ P1, K1, rep from ★ to within 2 sts of st at point of V, P2 tog, P1, P2 tog tbl, rib to end.
2nd row. Rib to within 2 sts of st at point of V, sl 1, K1, p.s.s.o., K1, K2 tog, rib to end.
Work 6 more rows in rib, at the same time dec in this way on every row.
Cast off in rib, dec as before.
Join left shoulder and neck border seam.
Place a marker 26(26:27:27)cm [10¼(10¼:10¾:10¾)in.] on each side of shoulder seams to mark depth of armholes.
Join cast off edge of sleeves to armhole edges.
Join side and sleeve seams.
Press seams.

MATERIALS

Poppleton Plaza D.K.

1st shade 801 Alabaster	3:	3:	4:	4:	50g balls
2nd shade 861 Alumina	7:	8:	9:	9:	50g balls

Pair each 3¾mm and 5mm knitting needles.

MEASUREMENTS

To fit chest	97:	102:	107:	112:	cm
	38:	40:	42:	44:	in.
Actual measurements	107:	112:	117:	122:	cm
	42:	44:	46:	48:	in.
Length	65:	65:	68:	68:	cm
	25½:	25½:	26¾:	26¾:	in.
Sleeve seam	50:	50:	51.5:	51.5:	cm
	19¾:	19¾:	20¼:	20¼:	in.

TENSION

22 sts and 28 rows = 10cm [4in.] over patt on 5mm needles.

ABBREVIATIONS

K = knit; P = purl; st(s) = stitch(es); A = 1st shade; B = 2nd shade; M1 = inc 1 st by picking up strand between last st worked and next st, and work into back of it; rep = repeat; tog = together; patt = pattern; tbl = through back of loop; inc = increase; cm = centimetres; in. = inches.

BACK

With 3¾mm needles and A, cast on 96(102:106:112) sts.
Work 7cm [2¾in.] in K1, P1, rib.
Next row. Rib 2(5:3:6), M1, * rib 4, M1, rep from * to last 2(5:3:6) sts, rib 2(5:3:6). [120(126:132:138) sts.]
Break off A and join in B.

Change to 5mm needles and 1st patt.
1st row. K1, * K2 tog and leave on needle, K again into the first st, slip both sts off the needle tog, rep from * to last st, K1.
2nd row. P.
3rd row. K2, rep from * as 1st row to last 2 sts, K2.
4th row. P.
These 4 rows form patt.
Work until back measures 44(44:47:47)cm [17¼(17¼:18½:18½)in.] from commencement, ending with a 2nd row.
Break off B and join in A.

Commence 2nd patt.
1st row. K1, * take right-hand needle behind the first st on left-hand needle and K the 2nd st tbl, then K the first st, slip both sts off the needle tog, rep from * to last st, K1.
2nd row. P.
3rd row. K2, rep from * as 1st row to last 2 sts, K2.
4th row. P.
These 4 rows form patt.
Work 26 more rows.
Break off A.
Join in B and work 18 rows in 1st patt.
Break off B.
Join in A and work 10 rows in 2nd patt.
Cast off.

LOOSE DIAGONAL

FRONT

Work as back.

SLEEVES

With 3¾mm needles and A, cast on 48(48:50:50) sts, and work 7cm [2¾in.] in rib as back.
Next row. Rib 4(4:3:3), M1, ★ rib 3, M1, rep from ★ to last 5(5:2:2) sts, rib 5(5:2:2). [62(62:66:66) sts.]
Break off A and join in B.

Change to 5mm needles and 1st patt as back.
Work 4 rows.
Now working the new sts in patt, inc 1 st at each end of next row, and then every 4th row until 116(116:122:122) sts are on the needle.
Work 1 row.
Break off B and join in A.
Work 10 rows in 2nd patt as back, inc on 3rd and following 4th row.
Cast off.

MAKING UP

Press each piece lightly, following instructions on ball band.
Join shoulder seams, leaving neck open as required.
Place a marker 28(28:29:29)cm [11(11:11½:11½)in.] on each side of shoulder seams to mark depth of armholes. Join cast off edge of sleeves to armhole edges.
Join side and sleeve seams.
Press seams.

Picture opposite: **Loose Diagonal** sweater in Poppleton Plaza Double Knitting wool

FOR PATIENT BEGINNERS

MATERIALS

Wendy Capri shade 170 Raffia 11: 12: 50g balls

Pair each 3¼mm and 4mm knitting needles. A medium crochet hook.

MEASUREMENTS

To fit chest	96/102:	104/109:	cm
	38/40:	41/43:	in.
Actual measurements	108:	116:	cm
	42½:	45½:	in.
Length	65:	65:	cm
	25½:	25½:	in.
Sleeve length	48:	48:	cm
	19:	19:	in.

TENSION

20 sts and 32 rows = 10cm [4in.] over
st. st. on 4mm needles.

ABBREVIATIONS

K = knit; P = purl; st(s) = stitch(es);
st. st. = stocking stitch; rep = repeat; M1
= inc 1 st by picking up strand between
last st worked and next st, and work in
to back of it; beg = beginning; alt =
alternate; dec = decrease; inc = increase;
d.c. = double crochet; cm = centimetres;
in. = inches.

FRONT

** With 3¼mm needles cast on
100(108) sts.
1st row. P1, K2, * P2, K2, rep from * to
last st, P1.
2nd row. K1, P2, * K2, P2, rep from * to
last st, K1.
Rep 1st and 2nd rows 6 times more, and
then 1st row once.

Change to 4mm needles.
Next row. P8(12), M1, * P12, M1, rep
from * to last 8(12) sts, P to end.
[108(116) sts.]

Continue in patt.
1st to 18th rows. Work in st. st., starting
with a K row.
19th row. K10(14), P30, K28, P30,
K10(14).
20th to 38th rows. Work in st. st.,
starting with a P row.
39th row. K36(40), P36, K36(40).
40th to 64th rows. Work in st. st.,
starting with a P row.
65th row. K2(6), P20, K42, P30, K14(18).
66th to 84th rows. Work in st. st.,
starting with a P row.
85th row. K31(35), P56, K21(25).
86th to 104th rows. Work in st. st.,
starting with a P row.
105th row. K12(16), P32, K20, P28,
K16(20).
106th to 115th rows. Work in st. st.,
starting with a P row.

Shape armholes.
Work in st. st., cast off 3 sts at beg of
next 4 rows. [96(104) sts.]
Work 3 rows.
123rd row. K54(58), P34, K8(12).
124th to 138th rows. Work in st. st.,
starting with a P row.
139th row. K36(40), P44, K16(20).
140th to 154th rows. Work in st. st.,
starting with a P row.
155th row. K3(7), P28, K65(69).
156th to 163rd rows. Work in st. st.,

starting with a P row. **

Commence yoke.
1st row [wrong side]. K1, P2, ★ K2, P2, rep from ★ to last st, K1.
2nd row. P1, K2, ★ P2, K2, rep from ★ to last st, P1.
Rep 1st and 2nd rows 5 times more.

Shape neck.
Next row. Rib 41(45) sts, cast off 14 sts, rib to end.
Continue on last set of sts, leaving remainder on a spare needle.
Work 1 row.
★★★ Cast off at beg of next and following alt rows 3 sts once, and 2 sts 3 times.
Work 1 row.
Dec 1 st at beg of next and following alt rows until 28(32) sts remain.★★★
Work 2 rows.
Cast off in rib.
With right side facing, rejoin yarn to remaining sts at neck edge, and follow instructions for other side from ★★★ to ★★★.
Work 3 rows.
Cast off in rib.

BACK

Follow instructions for front from ★★ to★★.

Commence yoke.
Work 24 rows in rib as front.

Shape back of neck.
Next row. Rib 36(40) sts, cast off 24 sts, rib to end.

Continue on last set of sts.
Work 1 row.
Cast off 5 sts at beg of next row and 3 sts at beg of following alt row.
Work 2 rows.
Cast off in rib.
With right side facing rejoin yarn to remaining sts at neck edge.
Cast off 5 sts at beg of next row, and

3 sts at beg of following alt row.
Work 3 rows.
Cast off in rib.

SLEEVES

With 3¼mm needles cast on 44(44) sts and work 21 rows in rib as front.

Change to 4mm needles.
Next row. P1, M1, P2, M1, ★ P3, M1, rep from ★ to last 5 sts, [P2, M1] twice, P1. [60 sts.]

Continue in patt.
1st to 18th rows. Work in st. st., starting with a K row, inc 1 st at each end of 6th, 12th and 18th rows.
19th row. K19, P32, K15.
20th to 30th rows. Work in st. st., starting with a P row, inc 1 st at each end of 23rd and 29th rows.
31st row. K8, P18, K14, P18, K12.
32nd to 50th rows. Work in st. st., starting with a P row, inc 1 st at each end of 35th, 41st and 47th rows.
51st row. K6, P12, K6, P22, K8, P16, K6.
52nd to 72nd rows. Work in st. st., starting with a P row, inc 1 st at each end of 53rd, 59th, 65th and 71st rows.
73rd row. K12, P44, K28.
74th to 92nd rows. Work in st. st., starting with a P row, inc 1 st at each end of 77th, 83rd and 89th rows.
93rd row. K49, P26, K15.
94th to 108th rows. Work in st. st., starting with a P row, inc 1 st at each end of 95th, 101st and 107th rows.
109th row. K8, P30, K58.
Continue in st. st., starting with a P row.
Work 3 rows.
Inc 1 st at each end of next row, and then the following 6th row. [100 sts.]
Work 7 rows.

Shape top.
Dec 1 st at each end of next row, and then the following 4th row.
Work 3 rows.
Cast off loosely.

FOR PATIENT BEGINNERS

MAKING UP

Press each piece lightly, following instructions on ball band.
Join shoulder, side and sleeve seams.
Sew sleeves into armholes.
Work a row of crab st along neck edge [1 row of d.c. but working from left to right instead of from right to left].
Press seams.

MATERIALS

Jaeger Luxury Spun Double Knitting with Alpaca
Shade 421 Primrose   16 × 50g balls

Pair each 3¾mm and 5mm knitting needles. A cable needle.

MEASUREMENTS

To fit chest	102/110:	cm
	40/43:	in.
Actual measurements	119:	cm
	47:	in.
Length	68:	cm
	26¾:	in.
Sleeve length	40:	cm
	15¾:	in.

TENSION

30 sts and 30 rows = 10cm [4in.] over cable patt.
16 sts and 30 rows = 10cm [4in.] over garter st patt on 5mm needles.

ABBREVIATIONS

K = knit; P = purl; st(s) = stitch(es); rep = repeat; C10F [cable 10 front] = slip next 5 sts on to cable needle and hold at front, K5, then K5 from cable needle; C10B [cable 10 back] = slip next 5 sts on to cable needle and hold at back, K5, then K5 from cable needle; patt = pattern; beg = beginning; sl 1 = slip 1; p.s.s.o. = pass slipped stitch over; tog = together; dec = decrease; alt = alternate; inc = increase; cm = centimetres; in. = inches.

BACK

** With 3¾mm needles cast on 85 sts.
1st row. K2, * P1, K1, rep from * to last st, K1.
2nd row. * K1, P1, rep from * to last st, K1.
Rep 1st and 2nd rows for 9cm [3½in.], ending with 1st row.
Next row. Rib to end, working twice into each st. [170 sts.]

Change to 5mm needles and patt.
1st row. K1, [K2, P1, K2, P2, K10, P2] twice, [K2, P1, K2, P2, K20, P2] 3 times, [K2, P1, K2, P2, K10, P2] twice, K2, P1, K3.
2nd row. K1, [K2, P1, K4, P10, K2] twice, [K2, P1, K4, P20, K2] 3 times, [K2, P1, K4, P10, K2] twice, K2, P1, K3.
3rd to 6th rows. Rep 1st and 2nd rows twice.
7th row. K1, [K2, P1, K2, P2, C10F, P2] twice, [K2, P1, K2, P2, C10B, C10F, P2] 3 times, [K2, P1, K2, P2, C10F, P2] twice, K2, P1, K3.

8th row. As 2nd row.
These 8 rows form patt.
Work until back measures 41cm [16in.] from commencement, ending with a wrong side row. **

Shape armholes.
Cast off 2 sts at beg of next 2 rows.
3rd row. K3, sl 1, K1, p.s.s.o., patt to last 5 sts, K2 tog, K3.
4th row. P3, patt to last 3 sts, P3.
5th row. K3, patt to last 3 sts, K3.
6th row. As 4th row.
Continue to dec in this way within the 3 sts at each end of next row, and then every 4th row until 126 sts remain.
Work 3 rows. Cast off, knitting 2 tog right along the row.

FRONT

Follow instructions for back from ** to **.

Shape armholes and neck.
Next row. Cast off 2 sts, patt 83 sts including st on needle, turn leaving remaining sts on spare needle.

Continue on these sts.
Work 1 row.
Next row. K3, sl 1, K1, p.s.s.o., patt to last 2 sts, K2 tog.
Continue to dec within the 3 sts for armhole, and 1 st at neck edge on every 4th row until 53 sts remain.
Now continue to dec for armhole on every 4th row, and at the same time, dec 1 st at neck edge on every alt row until 38 sts remain.
Work 3 rows.
Cast off, knitting 2 tog right along the row.
With right side facing, rejoin yarn to remaining sts and patt to end.
Next row. Cast off 2 sts, patt to end.
Next row. K2 tog, patt to last 5 sts, K2 tog, K3.
Complete to match other side.

SLEEVES

With 3¾mm needles cast on 45 sts.
Work 9cm [3½in.] in rib as back, ending
with 1st row.
Next row. * K1, work twice into each of
next 3 sts, rep from * to last st, K1.
[78 sts.]

Change to 5mm needles and patt.
1st row. K2, [K2, P1, K2] 5 times, P2,
K20, P2, [K2, P1, K2] 5 times, K2.
Continue in patt as set.
Work 11 more rows.
Now working the new sts in patt, inc 1 st
at each end of next row, and then every
14th row until 90 sts are on the needle.
Work until sleeve measures 40cm
[15¾in.] from commencement, ending
with a wrong side row.

Shape top.
Cast off 2 sts at beg of next 2 rows.
3rd row. K3, sl 1, K1, p.s.s.o., patt to last
5 sts, K2 tog, K3.
4th row. P3, patt to last 3 sts, P3.
5th row. K3, patt to last 3 sts, K3.
6th row. As 4th row.
7th row. As 3rd row.
8th row. As 4th row.
9th and 10th rows. As 7th and 8th.
Rep 3rd to 10th rows 7 times more.
[38 sts.]
Now continue to dec in this way at each
end of every alt row until 24 sts remain.
Work 13cm [5in.] without shaping for
shoulder saddle.
Cast off, knitting 2 tog right along the
row.

Neck border.
With 3¾mm needles cast on 181 sts.
1st row. K2, * P1, K1, rep from * to
last st, K1.
2nd row. * K1, P1, rep from * to last st,
K1.
Continue in rib.
Dec 1 st at each end of next row, and
then every alt row until 171 sts remain.
Work 1 row.
Inc 1 st at each end of next row, and
then every alt row until 181 sts are on
the needle.
Work 1 row.
Cast off in rib.

MAKING UP

Press each piece lightly, following
instructions on ball band.
Sew sleeves into armholes, and shoulder
saddles to shoulder edges.
Join side and sleeve seams.
Join shaped edges of neck border.
Place seam at point of V and sew border
to neck edge.
Fold in half and slip st in position.
Press seams.

MATERIALS

Phildar Pronostic

Main shade No. 80 Perle	10:	11:	12:	50g balls
Contrast shade No. 03 Atoll	1:	1:	1:	50g ball

Pair each 3mm and 3¾mm knitting needles. A cable needle.

MEASUREMENTS

To fit chest	97/102:	104/109:	112/117:	cm
	38/40:	41/43:	44/46:	in.
Actual measurements	107:	115:	122:	cm
	42:	45:	48:	in.
Length	62:	64:	65:	cm
	24½:	25¼:	25¾:	in.
Sleeve length	51:	51:	51:	cm
	20:	20:	20:	in.

TENSION

20 sts and 48 rows = 10cm [4in.] over 1st patt on 3¾mm needles.

ABBREVIATIONS

K = knit; K1B [K1 below] = insert right-hand needle into next st 1 row below and K it; M = main; C = contrast; P = purl; st(s) = stitch(es); rep = repeat; patt = pattern; M1 = increase 1 st by picking up strand between last st worked and next st, and work into back of it; st. st. = stocking stitch; C4F [cable 4 front] = slip next 2 sts on to cable needle and hold at front, K2, then K2 from cable needle; tog = together; dec = decrease; alt = alternate; inc = increase; cm = centimetres; in. = inches.

FRONT

** With 3mm needles and M, cast on 107(115:123) sts.
1st row. K2, * P1, K1, rep from * to last st, K1.
2nd row. * K1, P1, rep from * to last st, K1.
Rep 1st and 2nd rows for 6cm [2½in.], ending with 1st row.

**Change to 3¾mm needles and 1st patt.
1st row [wrong side].** K.
2nd row. K2, * K1B, K1, rep from * to last st, K1.
These 2 rows form patt.
Work until front measures 33(34:35)cm [13(13½:14)in.] from commencement, ending with 2nd row.
Next row. K3(7:1), M1, * K5(5:6), M1, rep from * to last 4(8:2) sts, K to end. [128(136:144) sts.]
Work 4 rows in garter st [every row K].
Now work 11 rows in st. st., starting with a K row.

Join in C.
With C, work 6 rows in garter st.
Break off C, and continue with M. **
Next row. K3(3:3), M1, [K7, M1] 3 times, K45(49:53), M1, [K7(7:8),M1] 8 times, K3(7:3). [141(149:157) sts.]
Continue as follows:
1st row. P1(5:2), [K4, P3] 10(10:11) times, K4, [P1, K1] 17(19:21) times, P1, [P3, K4] 4 times, P3.
2nd row. [K3, P4] 4 times, K3, P1, [K1, P1] 17(19:21) times, P4, [K3, P4] 10(10:11) times, K1(5:2).

3rd row. P1(5:2), [C4F, P3] 10(10:11) times, K4, [P1, K1] 17(19:21) times, P1, [P3, C4F] 4 times, P3.
4th row. As 2nd row.
Rep 1st to 4th rows 5 times more, and then 1st and 2nd rows once.
Next row. [K1, P1] 1(2:3) times, K2 tog, ★ [P1, K1] 3 times, P2 tog, [K1, P1] 3 times, K2 tog, ★ rep from ★ to ★ 3 times more, [P1, K1] 1(2:3) times, P1, K4, [P1, K1] 17(19:21) times, P1, [P3, C4] 4 times, P3.
Next row. Patt to last 62(66:70) sts, ★ P1, K1, rep from ★ to end. Continue in

moss st over the first 62(66:70) sts, keeping remainder in patt as before. Work until front measures 54.5(55:55)cm [21½(21¾:21¾)in.] from commencement, ending with a wrong side row.
Now work over the first 62(66:70) sts in garter st, keeping remainder in patt as before.
Work 8 rows.

Shape neck.
Next row. K54(58:62) sts, turn leaving remaining sts on spare needle.

Continue on these sts.
Dec 1 st at neck edge on next 9 rows, and then the 5 following alt rows.
Work 2 rows.
Cast off.
Rejoin yarn to remaining sts at neck edge, cast off 20 sts, work to end.
Complete to match other side.

BACK

Follow instructions for front from
** to **.
Next row. K.
Continue in st. st., starting with a K row.
Work until back is 6 rows less than front to shoulders.

Shape back of neck.
Next row. K45(49:53) sts, turn, leaving remaining sts on spare needle.
Continue on these sts.
Dec 1 st at neck edge on next 5 rows.
Cast off.
Rejoin yarn to remaining sts at neck edge, cast off centre 38 sts, work to end.
Complete to match other side.

SLEEVES

With 3mm needles and M, cast on 50(54:58) sts, and work 6cm [2½in.] in K1, P1, rib.
Next row. Rib 4(6:8), M1, ★ rib 7, M1, rep from ★ to last 4(6:8) sts, rib to end.
[57(61:65) sts.]
Change to 3¾mm needles.
Continue in 1st patt.
Work 8 rows.
Now working the new sts in patt, inc 1 st

at each end of next row, and then every 8th row until 77(81:85) sts, and then every 6th row until 109(113:117) sts are on the needle.
Work until sleeve measures 45cm [17¾in.] from commencement, ending with 2nd row.
Next row. K4, M1, ★ K5, M1, rep from ★ to last 5(4:3) sts, K to end.
[130(135:140) sts.]
Now work 4 rows in garter st, and 11 rows in st. st., and then with C, work 8 rows in garter st, and *at the same time* inc 1 st at each end of every 4th row.
[140(145:150) sts.]
Cast off.

MAKING UP

Press each piece lightly, following instructions on ball band. Join right shoulder seam.

Neck border.
With 3mm needles and M, pick up and K 21 sts down left side of front neck edge, 20 sts from the cast off sts, 21 sts up right side of neck and 52 sts along back neck edge.
Work 8 rows in K1, P1, rib.
Cast off in rib. Join left shoulder and neck border seam.
Place a marker 29(30:31)cm [11½(11¾:12)in.] on each side of shoulder seams to mark depth of armholes.
Join cast off edge of sleeves to armhole edges.
Join side and sleeve seams.
Press seams.

KNITTING NEEDLE SIZES

Original UK	000	00	0	1	2	3	4	5	6
Metric (mm)	9	8½	8	7½	7	6½	6	5½	5
USA	15	13	–	11	10½	10	9	8	7

Original UK	7	8	9	10	11	12	13	14
Metric (mm)	4½	4	3½ & 3¾	3¼	2¾ & 3	2½	2¼	2
USA	6	5	4	3	2	1	0	00

YARN SUPPLIERS

In case of difficulty, yarn may be ordered from the following sources:

AVOCET:
Avocet Hand Knitting Yarns
Hammond Associates Ltd
Hammerain House
Hookstone Avenue
Harrogate
North Yorkshire HG2 8ER
Tel: 0423 871481

BERGER DU NORD:
Viking Wools Ltd
Rothay Holme
Rothay Road
Ambleside
Cumbria LA22 0NZ
Tel: 0966 32991

FALKLAND ISLANDS TWEED:
Viking Wools Ltd
Address and telephone number as above

H.E.C. WOOLS:
Yeoman Yarns
89 Leicester Road
Kibworth
Leicestershire LE8 0HS
Tel: 053753 2351

JAEGER WOOLS:
Patons & Baldwins Ltd
P.O. Box
Darlington
Co. Durham DL1 1YQ
Tel: 0325 460133

Continued overleaf

LANG WOOL:

J. Henry Smith Ltd
Park Road
Calverton
Nottingham NG14 6LL
Tel: 0602 653131
(*Sole agent in UK for Lang yarns*)

PATONS & BALDWINS:

Patons & Baldwins Ltd
P.O. Box
Darlington
Co. Durham DL1 1YQ
Tel: 0325 460133

PHILDAR:

Phildar (UK) Ltd
4 Gambrel Road
Westgate Industrial Estate
Northampton NN5 5NF
Tel: 0604 583111/6

PINGOUIN:

French Wools Ltd
7–11 Lexington Street
London W1R 4BU
Tel: 01–439 8891

POPPLETON:

Richard Poppleton & Sons Ltd
Albert Mills
Hornbury
Wakefield WF4 5NJ
Tel: 0924 264141

SCHAFFHAUSER:

Smallwares Ltd
17 Galena Road
King Street
Hammersmith
London W6 0LU
Tel: 01–748 8511

SCHEEPJESWOL:

Scheepjeswol (UK) Ltd
P.O. Box 48
Unit 7
Colemeadow Road
North Moons Boat
Redditch
Worcestershire B98 9NZ
Tel: 0527 61056

WENDY WOOLS:

Carter & Parker (Wendy Wools) Ltd
Gordon Mills
Netherfield Road
Guiseley
Yorkshire LS20 9DT
Tel: 0943 72264